HOTSPOTS
MORO

CW00326373

Written by Conor Caffrey, updated by Ryan Levitt
Original photography by Debbie Stowe

Published by Thomas Cook Publishing
A division of Thomas Cook Tour Operations Limited
Company registration no. 1450464 England
The Thomas Cook Business Park, Unit 9, Coningsby Road,
Peterborough PE3 8SB, United Kingdom
Email: sales@thomascook.com, Tel: + 44 (0) 1733 416477
www.thomascookpublishing.com

Produced by Cambridge Publishing Management Limited
Unit 2, Burr Elm Court, Main Street, Caldecote, Cambs CB23 7NU
Series design based on an original concept by Studio 183 Limited

ISBN-13: 978-1-84157-859-0

First edition © 2006 Thomas Cook Publishing
This second edition © 2008
Text © Thomas Cook Publishing
Maps © Thomas Cook Publishing/PCGraphics (UK) Limited

Series Editor: Diane Ashmore
Production/DTP Editor: Steven Collins

Printed and bound in Spain by GraphyCems

Cover photography by Thomas Cook

Although every care has been taken in compiling this publication, and the contents
are believed to be correct at the time of printing, Thomas Cook Tour Operations
Limited cannot accept any responsibility for errors or omissions, however caused,
or for changes in details given in the guidebook, or for the consequences of any
reliance on the information provided. Descriptions and assessments are based on
the author's views and experiences when writing and do not necessarily represent
those of Thomas Cook Tour Operations Limited.

CONTENTS

WHAT'S IN YOUR GUIDEBOOK?

Independent authors Impartial up-to-date information from our travel experts who meticulously source local knowledge.

Experience Thomas Cook's 165 years in the travel industry and guidebook publishing enriches every word with expertise you can trust.

Travel know-how Contributions by thousands of staff around the globe, each one living and breathing travel.

Editors Travel-publishing professionals, pulling everything together to craft a perfect blend of words, pictures, maps and design.

You, the traveller We deliver a practical, no-nonsense approach to information, geared to how you really use it.

● *Town gate, Essaouira*

INTRODUCTION
Getting to know Morocco

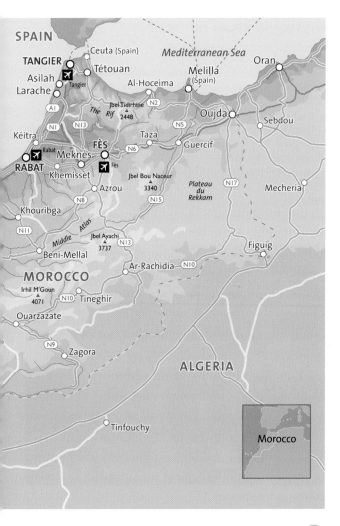

Getting to know Morocco

Morocco is the exotic land of the setting sun – *al-maghreb al-aqsa* in Arabic. Just a short hop from southern Spain and still with a considerable French and Spanish colonial influence, Morocco can at times seem almost European. At other times, its careful tradition reveals an Islamic nation at the heart of the Arab world.

Despite Morocco's evident Arab influence, its connection to the native Berber people remains strong. This is still a land on the edge of the world, inhabited by the spirits of the *jinn* (genie).

Morocco is a holiday destination for those with a sense of adventure. From the frenetic activity of its labyrinthian **Medinas** – the original, and often walled, Arab parts of the city – to the magic of its mountain, desert and coastal landscapes, it will captivate you and impel you to return again and again.

⬥ *Water sellers in Marrakech*

THE LAND

Morocco can be divided into four zones: the Atlantic and Mediterranean coastal regions; the desert that forms part of the Sahara; the great Middle and High Atlas Mountains that divide up the country, plus the Rif range to the north; and the great urban centres of the central plains. While the landscape is similar in some parts to southern Spain, many pockets remain quintessentially African.

THE PEOPLE

Most Moroccans are a mixture of Berber and Arab extraction, a result of centuries of assimilation between the two ethnic groups. Claims have been mooted that the Berbers, in North Africa since Neolithic times, are related to the Celts – so keep an eye out for redheads. Most Berbers nowadays are bilingual in Moroccan Arabic, the country's official language (along with French), and speak one of the three Berber dialects.

By the 8th century AD, the Arabs had brought Islam to Morocco, converting the Berber population. This influence is still seen today, and Islam is the official state religion. In recent times, migration from the rural countryside into the cities has become the most significant development to affect the Moroccan population, as the struggle to live on the land becomes increasingly difficult.

The hospitality of Moroccans is awe inspiring and if you go with the flow, there is every chance you will make some very good friends during your stay in the country.

THE HISTORY

As a main gateway between the African and European continents, Morocco has been invaded by a long list of foreigners throughout the ages, from the Phoenicians and Romans to relatively more recent and long-lasting incursions by the Arabs and Europeans. Moroccan independence from France and Spain came in 1956, when Sultan Mohammed V changed his title to that of king. However, remnants of this colonial past remain in the cuisine, architecture and language, creating a cosmopolitan mix of styles pleasing to the eye.

THE BEST OF MOROCCO

TOP 10 ATTRACTIONS

- **Beaches** Morocco's beaches are the best in North Africa. For **watersports** enthusiasts, this is heaven (see pages 64 and 102).

- **Kasbahs, oases and the desert** The great red kasbah forts that dominate the Moroccan oasis towns are a spectacle not to be missed (see pages 84 and 87).

- **Dinner in a palace restaurant in Meknès** Treat yourself to the sumptuous luxury of one of the palace restaurants in one of Morocco's greatest cities (see page 38).

- **Djemaa el Fna at night** Marrakech's greatest square transforms into a spectacle of the strange and wonderful. This is the ultimate street performance, where Carnival is every night (see page 49).

- **Shopping in the souks of Fès** Become pleasantly lost in the narrow streets of one of the medieval souks of Morocco's cities. Bargaining for souvenirs is great fun! (see page 42).

- **Street life in Casablanca** Moroccan cities are hustling, bustling places. Daily life is played out theatrically and the streets are the public arenas.

- **Riding in a calèche in Marrakech** They may scream 'tourist' but a horse-drawn carriage ride at sunset around the ramparts of Marrakech is an unforgettable experience (see page 52).

- **Designer decadence in Essaouira and Marrakech** Designers such as Yves Saint Laurent and numerous interior big-names have made this nation a second home. See how fashionistas put all the pieces together by avoiding a hotel in favour of a more intimate riad – the Moroccan version of a B&B.

- **Climb every Middle Atlas Mountain** Morocco may be a hotspot, but it's still possible to cool down in the stunning Atlas Mountains (see page 77).

- **Spot the stars in Ouarzazate** Ouarzazate is quickly becoming a second home to Hollywood A-listers. A large number of sizzling celebrities are bringing their talents to North Africa. See if you can get on set by arranging a tour at Atlas Studios (see page 57).

The beach at Cap Spartel near Tangier

SYMBOLS KEY
The following is a key to the symbols used throughout this book:

ⓐ address 🕿 telephone ⓕ fax ⓔ email ⓦ website address 🕒 opening times
❶ important

𝒊 information office		○ city	
✉ post office		○ large town	
🛍 shopping		○ small town	
✈ airport		▦ POI (point of interest)	
➕ hospital		═ motorway	
police station		— main road	
bus station		— minor road	
railway station		— railway	
✝ church			
❶ numbers denote featured cafés, restaurants & evening venues			

RESTAURANT CATEGORIES
Meals are rated according to the following guidelines. Please note, each rating is based on the cost of a main course for one person without drinks.
£ = up to £5   ££ = £5–£10   £££ = over £10

▶ *The Atlas Mountains of Morocco*

RESORTS
Places under the sun

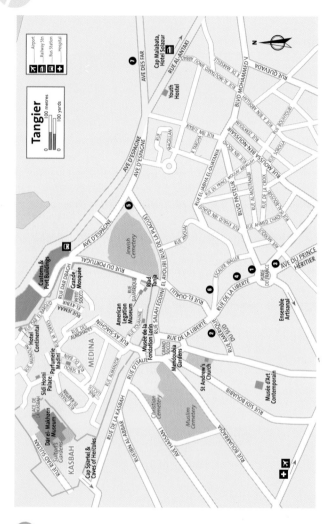

Tangier

0 — 100 metres
0 — 100 yards

✈ Airport
🚉 Railway Stn
🚌 Bus Station
✚ Hospital

N

Cap Malabata,
Hotel Mezazur

RUE AL ANTAKI

AVE DES FAR

BLVD MOHAMMED V

RUE QUEVADA

Youth
Hostel

RUE AL-MOUHAMAD RABOU ABBAS
RUE A'AIN TABAIN
RUE DE MARSEILLE

RUE EL MOUSSA BEN NOUSSAIR
RUE ZERKTOUNI
RUE IBN TUMAN
RUE MAGELLAN
RUE
MAGELLAN

AVE D'ESPAGNE

AVE D'ESPAGNE

AVE D'ESPAGNE

Jewish
Cemetery

🅿

RUE DU PORTUGAL

RUE EL JABHA EL OUATANIA
RUE DU PRINCE MOULAY ABDALLAH
RUE AHMED CHAOUKI
RUE KHALID IBN OUALID
RUE DE LA CROIX
BLVD PASTEUR
RUE AL-MOUTANABI
AVE MOKRI
RUE DE PASSO PARA
RUE ROGOID

Customs &
Port Buildings

RUE DAR DBAGH
PETIT SOCCO
EL-KTEBIR

Grande
Mosquée

Rbad
Tanja

RUE BANBIBA

RUE
BANBIBA

RUE EL-OUALILI

RUE DE LA PLAGE
RUE EL AYOUBI
RUE SALAH EDDINE

ESCALIER WALLER

AVE DU PRINCE
HÉRITIER

RUE
AMÉRICA

④

①

PARC DE FRANCE

Hôtel
Continental

American
Legation
Museum

RUE OUAHINE

RUE DE LA LIBERTE

⑥

RUE DE LA LIBERTE

RUE EMMA
RUE M TORRES

Musée de la
Fondation Loïn

GRAND SOCCO

Ensemble
Artisanal

MEDINA

RUE DU BAIN
SEBOU

RUE DES ALMOHADES

RUE D'ITALIE

RUE AS-SIACHIN

RUE DE LA LIBERTE

②

RUE DU SUD

RUE ALMANZOR

Parfumerie
Madini

Sidi Hosni
Palace

RUE DE KASBAH
RUE SIDI BOU ABID

Mendoubia
Gardens

St Andrew's
Church

RUE SIDI BOUABID

Musée d'Art
Contemporain

SOCCO

Christian
Cemetery

RUE DE LA KASBAH

Muslim
Cemetery

Dar el-Makhzen
Museum

Sultan's
Gardens

RUE IBN AL-ABBAR

AVE HASSAN

RUE BOUARAQIA

KASBAH

RUE RIAD SULTAN

Cap Spartel &
Caves of Hercules

PLACE DE
KASBAH

✈

✚

Tangier

A city with a bohemian past and the grandeur of a bygone era, Tangier, its lustre now slightly faded, remains a fascinating place to explore. Bustling and exciting, even quite seedy in parts, it is certainly not for the faint of heart.

In Tangier's heyday of the first half of the 20th century, residents were famous for their hell-raising antics and sense of fun. The city was well known as a place of cosmopolitan charm where the expatriate good life was lived to the full.

In this jet-setting time, anything went and it was said there was nothing one could not buy in its smoky bars and seedy souks. Artists and writers such as Beat poets Jack Kerouac and Allen Ginsberg flocked from America and Europe, drawn to the bohemian lifestyle. It was also a haven for the stylish and affluent 'Mediterranean set', where film stars casually rubbed shoulders with the criminal underworld and other unsavoury types.

Today's Tangier, a modern port with a large tourist trade, is more calm. Many of the insalubrious night-spots and seedy dens are long gone, sparkling apartment blocks and new resort hotels sprouting daily in their place. Locals good humouredly call themselves 'Tangerines', after the fruit that has been one of their more famous exports.

As Spain is very close – only 13 km (8 miles) across the Straits of Gibraltar – it acts as the gateway to Morocco for many tourists, who take the short hop over via the ferry (just over an hour). Be particularly careful of pickpockets and hustlers at the port entrance – fake guides will often lure tourists to shops or hotels they are paid a commission to take people to.

BEACHES

If you are not there already (most of the resort hotels are in this area), there is a mediocre town beach near Avenue des Far which continues on from the Avenue d'Espagne. Although the backdrop of white houses and the mountains is beautiful, the closer views of the busy port area are not very inspiring. Most of the beach is fairly clean, but the western end tends to be the most crowded and consequently the dirtiest. Attach yourself to a beach bar so that you can make use of one of the safer and more private changing cabins. Camel rides and hiring windsurfing equipment are two of the diversions on offer here; another is to watch the locals in their impromptu football matches or macho acrobatic performances on the sand.

If you go via hire car or taxi to the west of the town, there are some pleasant little sandy coves you can access not too far from the city, including **Jews' Beach**, named after the Spanish Jews who arrived on it after fleeing the Inquisition.

THINGS TO SEE & DO

American Legation Museum

A palace before it became the world's first American ambassadorial residence in 1777. Now a US National Monument, it houses an art gallery.
ⓐ Rue d'Amérique ⓣ 039 93 53 17 ⓛ 10.00–13.00 & 15.00–17.00 Mon–Fri

🔺 *Tangier Bay*

Cap Malabata, Cap Spartel and the Caves of Hercules

Tangier Bay is guarded by two promontories. To the east, Cap Malabata and its 19th-century lighthouse – which looks somewhat more like a medieval castle – guard the entrance to the Mediterranean, offering views back to Tangier and across to Algeciras in Spain. To the west, the wild and beautiful scenery of Cap Spartel marks the north-western tip of Africa. The beaches in the bay are decent, but can become crowded between July and August. The slightly touristy **Caves of Hercules** are nearby, and provide picturesque glimpses of the Atlantic Ocean. The best way to reach the promontories is by taxi or hire car. Try to arrange a day rate with the taxi driver before embarking.

ⓐ Next to the Mirage Hotel ⏱ 09.00–13.00 & 15.00–18.00 ❶ Admission charge

Grand Socco

A large circular market area that was a much livelier place in times past. Now it tends to be a hub of blue buses, taxis and myriad other traffic – automated and human. The market women who sit on the central patch of grass and peddle their wares add considerable colour to the proceedings with their wide-brimmed hats and red-striped cloths. Regeneration work was being done to the square at time of print so results are yet unknown.

Kasbah

A landmark in the city, with good views of the port. Once the location for the extravagant parties of movie stars and millionaires, this quarter includes luxury villas, as well as a **crafts and antiquities museum** in the 17th-century former Sultanate Palace. The Andalucian gardens are a highlight.

ⓐ North-east of the Medina, follow Rue Ben Raisouli to Place Amrah. The museum is in the Place de la Kasbah ☎ 039 93 20 97 ⏱ 09.00–12.30 & 15.00–17.30 Wed–Mon; closed Fri afternoon ❶ Admission charge

Musée de la Fondation Lorin

Explore the history of Tangier in this fascinating museum, housed in a former synagogue. Of special interest are the displays that chronicle

some of the city's more notable visitors, including Winston Churchill.
ⓐ 44 Rue Touahine 🕐 11.00–13.00 & 15.30–19.30 Sun–Fri

Parfumerie Madini

This perfumery is famed throughout North Africa for its scents, which are sold much cheaper than brand-name perfumes. It is the place to purchase essential oils, creams and potions – or have a special scent made to measure in front of you.
ⓐ 14 Rue Sebou (in the Medina) ☎ 039 93 43 88

Petit Socco and the Medina

This Medina is smaller than that of most other cities, and it is a bit rough and ready, so keep a tight hold on your belongings. Check out the colourful **Marché des Pauvres (Paupers' Market)** for bargains and the **Ensemble Artisanal** for leather goods and carpets. The central square is the **Petit Socco**, a somewhat seedy square with old cafés and hotels, famous for being the haunt of expats and film stars such as Errol Flynn and Cary Grant and the painter, Henri Matisse. The charm of the place is in its history.

Place de France

This square was once the hub of international intrigue during World War II. The spies may be all gone, but an atmosphere of nostalgic mystery lingers in the Café de Paris (see page 19).

St Andrew's Church

This is a beautiful and elegant little colonial English church. Famous expats – including the eccentric correspondent of *The Times*, Walter Harris, who lived in Morocco from the 1890s until his death in 1933 – are buried in the graveyard.
ⓐ Rue d'Angleterre 🕐 09.30–12.30 & 14.30–18.00

TAKING A BREAK

Café de Paris £ ❶ Another legacy of the colonial occupation.
ⓐ Place de France 🕐 06.00–23.00

Dean's Bar £ ❷ Built in 1837, this drinking den has played host to almost every traveller – both famous and not – who has ever passed through Tangier's city streets. ⓐ 2 Rue Amérique du Sud 🕐 09.00–23.00

Mix Max £ ❸ Popular fast-food establishment with a better-than-average menu selection and clientele. ⓐ 6 Avenue du Prince Héritier 🕐 12.00–23.00

Pâtisserie La Española £ ❹ Great cakes and pastries suitable for those after an elegant place to rest their feet after a full day of shopping and sightseeing. ⓐ 97 Rue de la Liberté 🕐 08.00–22.00

Restaurant Africa £ ❺ A friendly welcome and simple tasty Moroccan dishes await in this Spanish townhouse. ⓐ 83 Rue Salah Eddine El Ayoubi ☎ 039 93 54 36 🕐 10.00–23.00

Restaurant Populaire la Saveur de Poisson £ ❻ This unpretentious stall serves up the best fish in town. Featuring delicious sauces and spicings that combine the best of local seasonings, it's a great place for a casual bite or more filling meal. ⓐ 2 Escalier Waller 🕐 11.00–22.00 Sat–Thur

AFTER DARK

Pasarela ❼ A mass of bars and gardens combine in this large complex that even features an outdoor swimming pool. Summer brings out a number of regular live bands of varying quality. ⓐ Avenue des Far 🕐 20.00–03.00 Mon–Sat

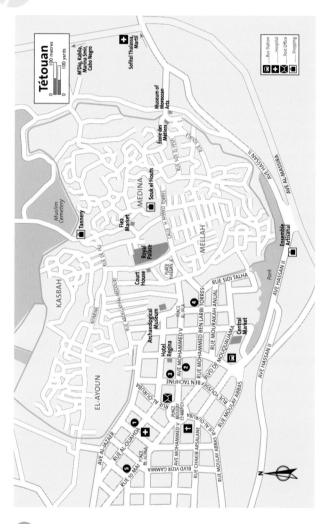

Tétouan

0   100 metres
0   100 yards

M'Diq, Kabila,
Marina Smir,
Cabo Negro

Sofitel Thalassa
Martil

Museum of
Moroccan
Arts

Muslim
Cemetery

Tannery

KASBAH

RUE DE FÈS

Flea
Market

École des
Métiers

MEDINA

Souk el Houts

RUE SIDI EL FEKI

CALLE H. HAMED TORRES

MELLAH

Royal
Palace

Court
House

PLACE
HASSAN II

RUE ABDELKHALAK TOBROUI

NTIRANE

RUE ABDALLAH MEDOURI

Archaeological
Museum

PLACE
AL JALA

RUE SIDI TALHA

AVE HASSAN II

Ensemble
Artisanal

Park

EL-AYOUN

Hotel
Regina

3

AVE MOHAMMED V

RUE AL-OUARDA

RUE MOHAMMED BEN LARBI TORRES

2

BLVD DE MOUQUAUAMA

RUE YOUSSEF BEN TACHFINE

RUE MOURAKAH ANUAL

Central
Market

AVE HASSAN II

AVE AL-MASSIRA

AVE HASSAN II

4

1

PLACE
MOULAY
EL HASSAN

AVE MOHAMMED V

AVE AL-OURUBA

RUE AL-OURUBA

RUE CHAKIB ARSALANE

BLVD VIZIR GAMMIA

RUE MOULAY ABBAS

RUE MOULAY ABBAS

AVE ALJAZAER

5

N

Bus Station
Hospital
Post Office
Shopping

20

Tétouan

The capital of Spanish Morocco until 1956, Tétouan is still influenced by its time as a colony. Several street signs remain in Spanish, and many older residents still speak the language. Locals call their city 'the Andalucian' or 'the daughter of Granada', as many of its original inhabitants emigrated from Andalucia to Tétouan in the 15th century during the persecution of Muslims and Jews. The architecture is particularly detailed and depicts considerable Spanish influence.

THINGS TO SEE & DO

There is plenty to do around Tétouan, with some great beaches and a decidedly more relaxed feel.

Archaeological Museum
Mainly contains Roman artefacts, including statues and mosaics from the ancient Roman sites of Lixus and Volubilis (see pages 74 and 75).
ⓐ Avenue Al-Jazaer ⓑ 08.30–12.00 & 14.30–18.30 Mon–Fri
ⓘ Admission charge

Cabo Negro
This attractive headland cape juts out into the Mediterranean, with a great 18-hole golf course (ⓣ 039 97 83 03). It is also one of the best places to go horse riding.
ⓐ Just north of Tétouan ⓣ 039 97 80 75 (contact La Ferma)

École des Métiers (Handicrafts School)
Tétouan is justly renowned for its craftsmen working with wood, clay and mosaic and their products make good souvenirs (see Medina, page 22). This local school, in a converted palace, offers tours around the classrooms.
ⓐ Inside the Medina walls, opposite Bab el Okla (the Queen's Gate)
ⓣ 039 97 27 21 ⓑ 08.00–12.00 & 14.30–17.30 Mon–Thur and Sat; closed Aug ⓘ Admission charge

Marina Smir

This is a glittering marina with restaurants, and a great Aquafun water
park for the kids. The beach here has fine, white sand.

 In Restinga Smir, 8 km (5 miles) north of M'Diq

Martil

This former medieval port acts as Tétouan's city beach, with a long and
pristine stretch of sand.

 11 km (7 miles) east of Tétouan

M'Diq/Kabila

M'Diq is a small fishing port with a quaint little harbour. Nearby Kabila
is a Spanish-style resort.

 18 km (11 miles) from Tétouan on the N13

Medina

Tétouan is known for its woodcraft, pottery and mosaics. Hire a guide to take
you through the noisy souks, where you will find goods by local craftsmen,
dyers and tanners. **Souk el Houts** is a place to look out for, with its small
Berber market where local women sell red and white striped *foutas*,
distinctive traditional Riffian skirts. If you want to avoid haggling, go to the
nearby **Ensemble Artisanal** where there are fixed-price souvenirs on display.

 Avenue Hassan II

Museum of Moroccan Arts

Older works of art, with displays of marriage ceremonies, a Berber kitchen
and Jewish jewellery.

 Avenue Hassan II 039 97 05 05 08.30–12.00 & 14.30–18.00
Wed–Sat

TAKING A BREAK

Jenin £ ❶ Popular café for younger residents and romancers. 8 Rue
al-Ouahda 039 96 22 46 05.30–21.00

Restaurant Restinga £ ❷ Cheap restaurant with good local cuisine.
ⓐ 21 Avenue Mohammed V ⏰ 12.00–14.30 & 19.00–21.30

Snack Yousfi £ ❸ Huge sandwiches packed with salad and fillings. A great option for vegetarians. ⓐ Rue Youseff ben Tachfine ⏰ 10.00–24.00

Restaurant Saigon ££ ❹ A Spanish-Moroccan restaurant with an Eastern name. Try hearty spicy *harira* soup followed by paella. ⓐ 2 Rue Mohammed Ben Larbi Torres ⏰ Hours vary

AFTER DARK

Rue 10 Mai ❺ Not a bar, but an actual street. This road is the place to go if you're looking for alcohol. Packed with establishments, it isn't very welcoming and is filled with some of the town's less salubrious characters. ⓐ Rue 10 Mai

🔺 *Doorway arch in Tétouan*

Asilah

This perhaps is the most Iberian of Moroccan resort towns and is perfect for a relaxed holiday with few foreign tourists. You could conceivably be in a small Andalucian resort, with the whitewashed houses and wrought iron balconies. Asilah's bizarre claim to fame is through the bandit Er Raisuli, who kidnapped many people in the early 20th century, making them 'walk the plank' out of his palace window, to their death on the rocks below. British writer Walter Harris (see page 18) was among those who spent an anxious time in his dungeon. At present, the palace is closed to visitors.

BEACHES

The most popular beaches are actually to the north of the town and they do get crowded during the height of summer. Walk south past the ramparts, however, and you will find quiet, isolated and pristine stretches of sand.

THINGS TO SEE & DO

International Festival of Music and Culture
Held each year in August, this event features international acts. During the festival, colourful murals are painted on all of the town's whitewashed walls.

EXCURSIONS
Larache & Lixus
If based in Asilah, you could make the 40 km (25 mile) trip to Larache to see the Roman ruins at Lixus (see page 74).

Lixus itself is the site of the legendary 'Garden of Hesperides', where Hercules picked golden apples after slaying a local dragon. In Roman times it was a centre for the manufacture of anchovy paste. The remains of a Neptune mosaic in the baths are worth checking out, although the site is certainly not as impressive or well-maintained as the Roman ruins of Volubilis, near Fès.

🅐 Frequent buses leave Larache bus station to Asilah and Tangier; *grands taxis* (see page 119) from Asilah to Larache leave when full from Asilah's Avenue Moulay Ismail; bus no. 4 runs from the port in Larache along the beaches to the ruins at Lixus 🕒 Sunrise to sunset ❶ Admission charge

Monoliths of M'Soura

This place features an impressive circle of aligned standing stones, much like Stonehenge. M'Soura means 'holy place' in Arabic.

🅐 About 25 km (15½ miles) south of Asilah. The signposting can be hard to follow – take the N1 south of Asilah for 16 km (10 miles) then take the R417 for Tétouan; after about 4 km (½ mile) take the road marked El Yemeni; the ruins are off this road about 5 km (3 miles) further on.

TAKING A BREAK

Most of the better restaurants are around Place Zallach and the seafront area, many providing outdoor sittings.

Al-Madina ££ Enjoy a light dish selected from the simple menu of Moroccan faves. Outdoor seating facing a main square in the Medina makes it a great place for people-watching. 🅐 Place Abdellah Guennoun 🕒 Hours vary

Casa Garcia ££ Spanish-style restaurant. 🅐 51 Rue Moulay Hassan Ben Mehdi ❶ 039 41 74 65 🕒 Hours vary

Chez Pepe (El Oceano) ££ Fried fish and salad are mostly on the menu here. 🅐 8 Place Zallach ❶ 039 41 73 95 🕒 Hours vary

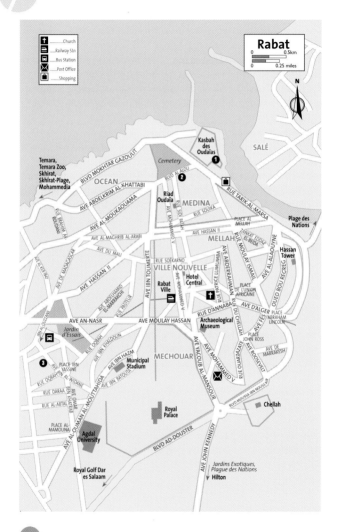

Rabat

At the mouth of the Bou Regreg River, this former Phoenician trading post first came to prominence under the Romans as their southernmost port – Sala Colonia. By the 17th century, the nearly ruined city was repopulated by Andalucian refugees, who rebuilt the kasbah and created their own pirate state, dominated by the infamous Salee Rovers. These corsairs (Barbery pirates) targeted European merchant ships, reaching as far afield as the British Isles. From 1912 to 1956, Rabat was the French Protectorate's administrative capital, and remains Morocco's capital today. Modern Rabat is a large city with wide boulevards and shaded streets and with an architecture that harks back to an era of French colonialism – the pirates are gone and old Sala is a suburb known as Salé.

BEACHES

This stretch of Atlantic coastline boasts some of Morocco's most exclusive beaches. **Temara** and **Skhirat-Plage** are the most popular and upmarket, with plenty of restaurants and nightclubs. These are safer waters for swimming than the northern shores of Rabat, but beware – Atlantic currents are treacherous. About 12 km (7½ miles) north of Rabat is the chic **Plage des Nations**, an awe-inspiring sweep of sand stretching as far as the eye can see. It may come as a surprise, given that it is highly industrial, but **Mohammedia** has some fine beaches, including one of the best beaches in Morocco, and plenty of interest for the tourist.

THINGS TO SEE & DO

Archaeological Museum

Filled with Roman treasures, with an impressive collection of bronzes from Volubilis.

ⓐ 23 Rue Al Brihi ⓣ 037 70 19 19 ⓛ 09.00–11.30 & 14.30–17.30 Wed–Mon
ⓘ Admission charge

⬥ *Entrance gate to Chellah Roman ruins*

Chellah

Possibly the most beautiful and romantic ruin in Morocco. Within the Merenid walls are the tombs of the Black Sultan and his wife, Morning Light, an Englishwoman who converted to Islam. White storks nest in the minaret of the mosque. There is also a sacred pool where – in the hope of becoming fertile and producing children – women feed the eels with eggs.

ⓐ Boulevard Moussa Ibn Noussair ⏱ 08.30–18.30 ❶ Admission charge

Ensemble Artisanal

Witness top craftsmen and artisans at this collection of workshops where you can see them at work and purchase the results. Choose from examples of tilework, embroidery, leather, brass and much more. You may not be able to enjoy the fun of bartering, but you'll know the quality of the goods is top-notch (if a little more expensive than usual).

ⓐ 6 Rue Tarik al Marsa ☎ 037 73 05 07 ⏱ 09.00–12.30 & 14.30–18.00

Golf

The **Royal Golf Dar Es Salaam**, Morocco's most famous course, is a blossoming golf oasis where green fees are much lower than in Europe. It includes two 18-hole and one 9-hole courses.

ⓐ 10 km (6 miles) outside Rabat, on Route des Zaers ☏ 037 75 58 64
ⓕ 037 75 75 71

Hassan Tower

This is all that remains of what – if it had been completed – would have been the second largest mosque in North Africa. Note that each face of the tower is different.

ⓐ Oued Bou Regreg ⏰ 08.00–16.00

Jardins Exotiques de Sidi Bouknadel

Created by a French horticulturist during the 1950s to display plants from Africa and Asia.

ⓐ Just before the beach at Temara ⏰ 09.00–18.30 ❶ Admission charge

Kasbah des Oudaïas

The kasbah sits guarding the estuary – its Bab (meaning gate), beautifully ornate with a repetitive palm-frond motif, is meant to inspire you to prayer.

Royal Palace

The official residence of the royal family cannot be entered, but it can certainly be admired. Most come to visit in order to get a picture taken with the ceremonial guards dressed in red and white who stand guard. Be sure not to stray too far from the main road that runs down the centre of the complex, otherwise you may find yourself removed from the area.

ⓐ Djemaa el Fas ☏ No phone

Salé

On the other side of the river in Salé, the atmosphere is remarkably different from Rabat's more refined city centre, becoming more suburban and dominated by residential areas. There are some fine mosques and *medersas* (religious schools), but note that some of these are out of bounds for non-Muslims. The market area of the **Mellah**, the old Jewish quarter, is a fascinating place for a wander. Look all you like – you will not find any pirates left in Salé!

ⓐ If you are walking, cross the river by the bridge opposite the Hassan Tower and enter the Salé Medina via the main gate at Bab Mrisa (Port Gate); otherwise, go to Salé by bus, taxi or rowing boat water taxi

Ville Nouvelle (New Town)
The location of government offices and foreign embassies. Just opposite the impressive colonial Parliament building, **Hotel Balima** was Morocco's first European-style hotel (1932) and is still the scene of political intrigue.

TAKING A BREAK

Café Maure £ ❶   Delightful place under the fig trees, overlooking the estuary. Delicious pastries. ⓐ Kasbah des Oudaïas 🕐 09.00–17.30

Dinarjat £££ ❷   The best Moroccan restaurant in town. ⓐ 6 Rue Belgnaoui, Medina 🕿 037 70 42 39 🕐 Lunch and dinner; hours vary ❶ Accepts major credit cards

AFTER DARK

5th Avenue ❸   If a Moroccan had designed New York City, then this is what America's metropolis would look like. The music selections are eclectic, which makes it even more intriguing. ⓐ 4 Ave Bin al-Widane 🕿 037 77 52 54 🕐 22.00–05.00 Sat & Sun

Casablanca

Those expecting the filmic romance of Humphrey Bogart and Ingrid Bergman will be disappointed with a trip to Casablanca. Although it put the city on the map, the film wasn't made locally, and the 'exotic orientalism' it portrayed doesn't really exist here. Casa, as the locals call it, is a modern industrial city, a sprawling metropolis of about 3 million people, forming Africa's second largest city after Cairo. Yet there is much more to the city than this, and visitors will find it well worth the stay.

Casa is also the most European of North African cities, with wide boulevards and extensive Mauresque and art deco architecture. Visitors here will also find good-quality accommodation, some of Morocco's best restaurants and one of the country's quieter Medinas, the perfect place to pick up souvenirs and craft items. The elegant Hassan II Mosque – the world's second-largest mosque, with a massive prayer hall – is the city's newest emblem.

However, it is also worth noting that visitors on more than a day trip to Casa will see two sides to the city – one of riches and one of desperation. While the salubrious suburb of Anfa exudes comfortable wealth, it is surrounded by a sea of inconspicuous rundown apartments and *bidonvilles*, or shantytowns.

BEACHES

Aïn Diab is the best beach in the city and well-recommended. About 3 km (2 miles) from town, it stretches for about the same distance. The beach itself is not exciting; better to use one of the swimming pool complexes or beach clubs that stretch along the coast – they have daily rates for usage, which vary in price. The pools contain filtered seawater and there is a wide range of other facilities, from cafés and restaurants to nightclubs. At the weekend, impromptu football games are set up by local kids on the beach.

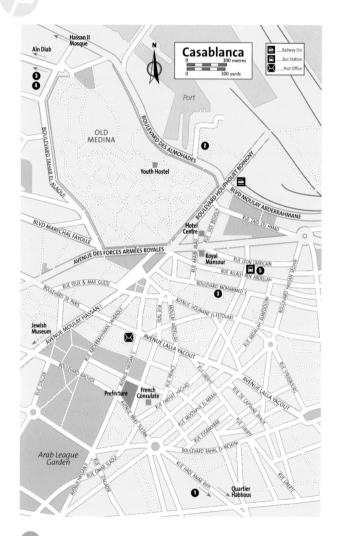

THINGS TO SEE & DO

Aïn Diab

A corniche road leads from Casablanca city centre to Aïn Diab, the main resort area. A pre-dinner evening stroll along the *Corniche* (clifftop road) here is recommended – it tends to be a parade of Moroccan well-to-do families and provides for some good people-watching.

ⓐ 3 km (2 miles) south along the Corniche; take bus no. 9 from Boulevard de Paris

Arab League Garden

Rows of palm trees line this shady park in the centre of the city – a quiet place to sit, sip tea in one of the cafés and admire the rose bushes.

ⓐ South of Place Mohammed V

Colonial buildings

Place Mohammed V is the centrepoint of Casablanca and is the focus of some fine colonial architecture. The local Mauresque architecture is a mix of art deco colonial and local Moorish influences. Look out for the **French Consulate**, the grand **Post Office** and the **Prefecture**. In the square itself is a musical fountain that is meant to light up and sing at night, but which doesn't always do so.

Hassan II Mosque

Arguably the most spectacular mosque in the Islamic world. For those who have never seen the interior of a mosque, this is the opportunity to take a tour because it is one of the few mosques in Morocco that non-Muslims are permitted to enter. There is an electronic roof that can open and close.

ⓐ Boulevard Sidi Mohammed Ben Abdallah; access by *petit taxi*

ⓣ 022 48 28 86 ⓛ Open to non-Muslims for guided tours only 09.00, 10.00, 11.00 & 14.00 Sat–Thur ⓘ Admission charge

Jewish Museum

The only museum to Jewish culture in an Islamic country, this is a fascinating insight into Casablanca's considerable Jewish population. ⓐ 10 km (6 miles) out of town, 81 Rue Chasseur Jules Gros ⓣ 022 99 49 40 ⓛ 10.00–17.00 Mon–Fri ⓘ Admission charge

Old Medina

The Portuguese first settled on this coast in the 15th century. When they returned in the 16th century they named their port Casa Blanca – the White House. This settlement, on a small hill above the bay, was destroyed by the Lisbon earthquake of 1755, and it was not until Arab merchants began to settle in the 19th century that its ruins were cleared and a Medina built. Today, the Medina is sparsely populated and offers little in the way of traditional crafts, although it is a pleasant place for a walk.

⬥ *Casablanca's impressive Hassan II Mosque*

Quartier Habbous

The Habbous quarter is a great place for a stroll, with the most relaxed and easy-going Medina in Morocco. There are some good shops where you are guaranteed to pick up souvenir treasures.

ⓐ Boulevard Victor Hugo; access by bus no. 4 or 40 from Boulevard de Paris, or by *petit taxi*

TAKING A BREAK

Pâtisserie Bennis Habous £ ❶ The best place for tasty Moroccan pastries and coffee, to replenish your energies for shopping in the New Medina. ⓐ 2 Fkih El Gabbas ❶ 022 30 30 25 ❶ 08.00–20.00

Port de Pêche ££ ❷ Great for seafood paella, *tajines* (see page 96) and fish soup. ⓐ Le Port de Pêche ❶ 022 31 85 61 ❶ Lunch and dinner; hours vary ❶ Accepts major credit cards

À Ma Bretagne £££ ❸ Morocco's most famous French restaurant, with a great ocean view, and serving a dazzling array of fish and seafood. The high standard is matched by the price. ⓐ Aïn Diab, Boulevard de la Corniche ❶ 022 36 21 12 Ⓦ www.amabretagne.com ❶ 18.30–22.00 Mon–Sat; closed Aug ❶ Accepts major credit cards

AFTER DARK

La Petite Roche ❹ Soak up the views of Hassan II Mosque from the comfort of this restaurant/bar. Local movers and shakers often start their nights on the town here. ⓐ Boulevard de la Corniche ❶ 022 39 57 48 ❶ Hours vary

La Bodéga £ ❺ Tuck into light nibbles or sip on a beer or two while you dance the night away to the mish-mash of both local and international tunes. ⓐ 129 Rue Allah ben Abdellah ❶ 022 54 18 42 ❶ 12.30–15.00 & 19.00–24.00

Meknès

Meknès, not really on the tourist trail, is an interesting place to spend a few days, and is less frenetic than other Moroccan cities in the vicinity. Located in the middle of an agricultural area, it is divided by the River Boufekrane into the old Medina and the newer French Ville Nouvelle.

Moulay Ismail, one of the most powerful Moroccan sultans, wanted to make Meknès as magnificent as Versailles in France and extravagantly built over 50 palaces here. Many are ruins but remain fascinating and other monuments are being restored. Meknès is about an hour and a half from Fès by car – at least a half-day trip if you make an early start. You could spend a more leisurely few days here if you make it your base.

THINGS TO SEE & DO

Bab Mansour

An incredibly ornate gateway and a city icon. Apparently the El Mansour who built it was asked by the Sultan if he could do better and he replied he could. Unfortunately, the Sultan sought perfection and the architect was immediately executed.

ⓐ Place el Hedim

Dar Jamai Museum

Excellent museum with displays of ceramics, carpets and jewellery.

ⓐ Place el Hedim ❶ 055 53 08 63 ⏱ 09.00–13.00 & 15.00–18.30
❶ Admission charge

Heri as Souani

The Royal Granaries aren't very interesting aesthetically, but they are a true tribute to the greatness of Moulay Ismail – the second Alouite Sultan. Designed to hold enough grain to feed all 12,000 houses within the city walls over a 20-year period in case of siege, it prevented grain rotting due to the ingenious cooling system involving the installation of

● *Bab Mansour – one of several elaborate gates in Meknès*

a reservoir underneath and the planting of a forest on the roof.
ⓐ Heri as Souami ● No phone ● 09.00–13.00 & 15.00–18.30

Imperial City
By the 17th century Meknès boasted over 50 palaces, but most are now
pretty much in ruins.
ⓐ South-east of Place Lalla Aouda ● Open access

Medersa Bou Inania
This 14th-century religious school boasts intricate decorative interiors
and unique minarets inlaid with bands of green tiles.
ⓐ Souk es Sebat ● 09.00–13.00 & 15.00–18.30 ● Admission charge

Medina
You will find few tourists in this authentic Medina, which has
traditional *qissaria*, or covered markets. The elegant Place El Hedime has

a particularly colourful food market, where you will doubtless find fresh mint, for which Meknès is famous throughout Morocco. For more durable souvenirs, try Rue Sebat, where you will find the stores peddling the more tourist kind of wares.

TAKING A BREAK

Les Palmiers d'Aziza £ Dig into the scrumptiously sweet treats at this soothing café complete with a garden and bubbling fountains. A great place to rest your feet or catch up with friends. **ⓐ** 9 Rue de Tarfaya **ⓣ** No phone **ⓛ** 06.00–24.00

Restaurant Riad/Palais Didi ££ Small garden restaurant with a Moroccan menu. **ⓐ** 79 Ksar Chaacha, Dar Kebira **ⓣ** 055 53 05 42 **ⓛ** Lunch and dinner; hours vary **ⓘ** Accepts major credit cards

Restaurant Zitouna ££ Traditional fare in a 19th-century Moroccan house. Popular restaurant with coach tours, but quieter and more relaxed in the evenings. **ⓐ** 44 Jamaa Zitouna **ⓣ** 055 53 02 81 **ⓛ** Lunch and dinner; hours vary **ⓘ** Unlicensed

Collier de la Colombe £££ Modern restaurant with a varied menu. The trout is recommended. **ⓐ** 67 Rue Driba, Medina – near Place Lalla Aouda **ⓣ** 035 55 50 41 **ⓛ** Lunch and dinner; hours vary **ⓘ** Licensed; accepts major credit cards

AFTER DARK

Discotheque el Andalouse If you're really yearning for a chance to dance the night away, then this disco – located in the Hotel Bab Mansour – is probably your best bet. Otherwise, save your dirhams and spend them instead at the numerous live music venues in bars such as the Transatlantique and Rif. **ⓐ** 38 Rue el-Emir Abdelkader **ⓣ** 035 52 52 39 **ⓛ** 22.00–04.00

Fès

Fès is a wonderfully mystical city that seems trapped in medieval times.
For centuries it has been the centre of Islam in Morocco and contains
one of the most important religious schools and the world's oldest
university. For visitors, it is a place filled with mystery as you wonder
about the life conducted behind the veil of closed doors. While those
walking in the Medina will only catch glimpses of the hidden Fès,
it will stir the imagination much more than a full picture.

The city is divided into three distinct parts: **Fès el Djedid (New City)**, **Fès
el Bali (Old City)** and **Ville Nouvelle**, to the south. Fès el Djedid, built as a
planned city some distance from old Fès in the 13th century, was joined to
Fès el Bali in the 19th century. While it has a distinctive feel and character,
it is often neglected by tourists, who instead flock to the maze of the Old
City. Further south, the modern and very European district of Ville Nouvelle,
built by the French during colonial rule, has good cafés and shopping. The
traditional early evening promenade is a must for those who like to strut
their stuff before they head out to eat in the evening.

To get some semblance of direction in the disordered and confusing
medieval maze that is Fès el Djedid, it is wise to hire an official guide for
your first venture into the Medina. Your hotel or the tourist information
office will recommend one. Fès' Medina – now a UNESCO-protected
heritage site – is extremely important to Moroccan Muslims and the rest
of the Islamic world, renowned as a place of ancient religious learning.
Its university is attached to the Kairouiyne mosques and *medersas*, the
religious schools of instruction. For non-Muslims, who are not permitted
entry to most of these sights, this Islamic world remains hidden. But the
old city is also the place for souvenir hunting, where craftsmanship
excels in the souks and *fondouks* (workshops). Hustling and haggling are
part of Medina life, but this is not a dangerous place.

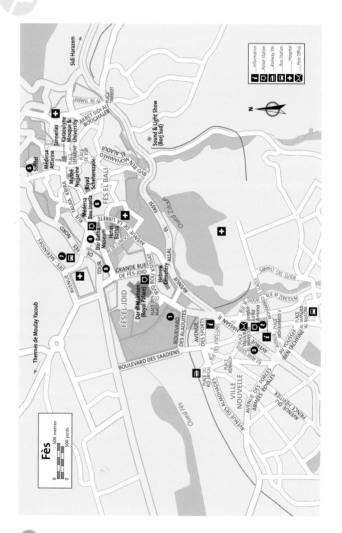

THINGS TO SEE & DO

Carpet shops

A visit to a carpet shop is a must during your stay in Fès, but remember that you will be under no obligation to buy. The sales pitch will be laid on thick, and it is slick, but you will see some truly beautiful carpets, learn something about how they are made and drink a glass or two of delicious mint tea. If you want to buy, **Au Merveille du Tapis** is one of the more reputable shops.

ⓐ Rue Sebaa Louyet, off Place Seffarine

Dar Batha Museum

Set in a sumptuous palace, this museum provides an excellent introduction to Moroccan traditional arts and crafts.

ⓐ Place de l'Istiqlal ⓣ 055 63 41 16 ⓛ 08.30–11.45 & 14.30–18.00 Wed–Mon ❶ Admission charge

Dar el Makhzen (Royal Palace)

Closed to the public, but the ornate entrance gate is a feast of opulent design.

ⓐ Place des Alaouites

Dyers' souk and tanneries

Bubbling pots of colour make the dyers' souk – Souk Sabbighin – one of the city's most colourful places, where wool and cotton hang out to dry and leather skins are dipped in the vats by men in shorts. Despite the pungent smell, it is a mesmerising sight.

Karaouiyne Mosque

Non-Muslims are not allowed to enter this mosque, founded in 857 AD, which contains the world's oldest university. You are only permitted a glimpse through the spectacular ornate gates.

ⓐ East of Souk Attarine

Medersas

The *medersas* of Fès have some of the most beautifully decorated tilework and wood carving imaginable, with tile designs, called *zellig*, in distinctive patterns that are not meant to distract but to entice the faithful to pray and fill them with thoughts of the divine. The best examples of this are **Medersa Attarine** (ⓐ Opposite Karaouiyne Mosque 🕐 09.00–13.00 & 15.00–18.30 ❶ Admission charge) and **Medersa Bou Inania** (ⓐ Near Bab Bou Jeloud on Rue Talaa Kebira 🕐 09.00–17.00 ❶ Admission charge).

Mellah

Although there are now few Jewish inhabitants in Fès, several synagogues and 18th- and 19th-century houses remain. The **Hebrew Cemetery** is filled with white tombs.
ⓐ East of Place des Alaouites 🕐 07.00–19.00 ❶ Donation expected

Musée Nejjarine

It's hard to know what is more impressive – the displays of crafts and woodworking or the building the museum is located in. Housed in a restored caravanserai for travelling artisans and merchants, it is a beautiful collection of some of the best examples of local artistry offering up everything from wooden chests and furniture to religious artefacts.
ⓐ Place an-Nejjarine ☎ 035 74 05 80 🕐 10.00–17.00

Souks and fondouks

The souks of Fès offer the finest, but not the cheapest, Moroccan crafts. A wander through the teeming streets is unforgettable. Yet this is not a mere tourist attraction; the Medina's souks have been here for centuries. You will see the craftsmen working away in their *fondouks*. Fès is particularly famous for its ceramics, but you will also find many other high-quality crafts and potential souvenirs.

Sound and Light Show

Fès' famous 'Son et Lumière' show is put on here.

🅐 Borj Sud – south of Boulevard Allal el Fassi ☎ 055 62 93 71, or contact the local tourist office or large hotels for details and to book 🕒 Oct–Mar

Spas

Morocco's curative waters have been exploited since Roman times. In the Middle Atlas Mountains, mineral-rich water springs forth from volcanic rock at a steady 54°C (130°F) with several spas taking advantage of the touted curative benefits. The luxurious **Thermes de Moulay Yacoub**, set amidst the rolling Trhrat hills, comprises hot water swimming pools, individual mineral baths, as well as relatively inexpensive massage and beauty treatments (🅐 20 km/12½ miles north-west of Fès; hire a taxi for the day ☎ 055 69 40 64). There are more old-fashioned spa baths at **Sidi Harazem**, a eucalyptus-covered shrine, dating from the 17th century, now well known for its healing mineral water (🅐 15 km/9 miles south-east of Fès).

FAUX GUIDES

Even though it is illegal to do so, some Moroccans will offer to guide you around Fès even though they are not qualified or authorised to do so. Only hire a guide who has been recommended to you by your hotel or by the tourist office.

Most *faux guides* will not cause you any harm, although there have been stories in the past of muggings and threats. The most likely scenario is that you will be frustrated by their lack of any knowledge of tourist sights and their insistence that you visit their 'brother's' souvenir shop. No matter how hard you bargain in this shop, you will pay an amount to include the *faux guide*'s commission.

Most Moroccan cities have tourist police who ensure *faux guides* are kept to a minimum and as soon as you mention them, the *faux guide* will likely disappear into thin air.

TAKING A BREAK

Fès is arguably the best place to eat in Morocco.

Café Restaurant la Noria £ ❶   Get away from the crazy streets of the city by pulling up a chair at this simple establishment located in the Bou Jeloud Gardens. If you're hungry, there is a small menu of tasty treats to choose from. ⓐ Fès el-Jdid ❶ No phone ● 07.00–21.00

Café Restaurant 24H £ ❷   Just as the name says, this establishment is open round the clock, serving up basic dishes such as sandwiches, salads and tajines. Its location in the central market means ingredients are always fresh. ⓐ Marché Central, Avenue Mohammed V ❶ 035 62 36 97 ● 24 hrs a day, seven days a week

Restaurant Bajelloul £ ❸   Whether it's a lunchtime snack or something later at night, this tasty sausage and kebab stall is sure to sate your appetite. Its late (well, late for Morocco) opening hours make it especially popular with young revellers. ⓐ Rue Arabie Saoudite ❶ No phone ● 12.00–24.00

Medina Café ££ ❹   Situated near the gate into the Medina, this café makes a great place to watch the world from. The Moroccan dishes on the menu are especially good. ⓐ 6 Derb Mernissi Bab Boujeloud ❶ 035 63 34 30 ● 07.00–22.00

Al Fassia £££ ❺   World-renowned Fassi cuisine in elegant surroundings, with a terrace overlooking the Medina and nightly Andalucian music. ⓐ Sofitel Palais Jamai, 21 Rue Salaj ❶ 035 63 73 14 ● 08.00–23.00

Dar Saada £££ ❻   A converted palace serving top-notch Moroccan food. Try lamb tajine with almonds. ⓐ 21 Souk Attarine ❶ 035 63 73 70 ● Lunch only ❶ Accepts major credit cards

🔺 *One of many French colonial-style tea and coffee houses in Fès*

AFTER DARK

Hôtel les Mérinides ➐ Everyone who's anyone kicks off their evening at this bar boasting a panoramic view over the city. Marvel over the cocktails and the view before you head off to less salubrious locales. ⓐ Route du Tour de Fès ⓣ 035 64 52 26 ⓛ 18.00–23.00 (hours vary if a large crowd stays late)

Jnan Palace Hotel ➑ Two venues in one. For something a bit quiet and cultural, head to the bar at this hotel to enjoy live acts playing local tunes. Otherwise, go over to the disco (Le Phoebus) if a raucous night of partying is more to your liking. ⓐ Avenue Ahmed Chaouki ⓣ 035 65 39 65 ⓛ 21.00–03.00

RESORTS

El Jadida

One of a series of former Portuguese colony ports, this is a relaxed place that is underdeveloped from a tourist perspective. A lot of Moroccans do come here, especially at the weekends in the summer when the beaches fill up. The Portuguese citadel forms the focus of the town and is in effect its Medina. With a grid shape that reflects its European design, it is relatively easy to navigate the streets, so you won't really need a guide. A large mosque with a pretty dome dominates the skyline.

BEACHES

The beaches around El Jadida can become crowded with Moroccan families from the cities of Marrakech and Casablanca during the summer, especially at the weekends. For hiring gear or getting lessons in surfing and windsurfing, contact **Club Nautique** at El Jadida port.

THINGS TO SEE & DO

Ancient city of Tit
Now called Moulay Abdullah, this ancient Berber city is the site of a large religious festival in September, when the place fills up with Berber tents. The ramparts of the city, with its fortified monastery, have been restored.
ⓐ 11 km (7 miles) from El Jadida

Azemmour
A small white Medina perched on the banks of the Oum er Rbia River, Azemmour was once an important fishing port that has now slipped into peaceful obscurity. It is a very pleasant and rewarding excursion from El Jadida. The terrace around the ramparts of the Kasbah offers views back towards Casablanca. Stretching south from the town, Azemmour's long sandy beach is excellent. There is a local market on Tuesday.
ⓐ 16 km (10 miles) north of El Jadida

Portuguese cistern
A very atmospheric underground cistern that was used in the Orson Welles film version of *Othello*. The few inches of water reflect the roof and pillars in this cool subterranean space.
ⓐ Rue Mohamed Al Ahchemi Bahbah ⓛ 09.00–13.00 & 15.00–18.30
ⓘ Admission charge

TAKING A BREAK

Patisserie Royale £ Fantastic breakfast and break spot serving up delicious morning meals or lunchtime bites. Get chatting to the couple next to you or sit and read a book – it's up to you. ⓐ Place Mohammed V
ⓣ 061 87 83 54 ⓛ 06.00–20.00

Restaurant Le Tit £ Sick of Moroccan food and just want a beer and something familiar to taste on your plate? This pub-like eatery will fit the bill. ⓐ 2 Avenue Al-Jamia El-Arabi ⓣ 023 34 39 08 ⓛ 09.00–24.00

AFTER DARK

Avenue Nabeul The bars and cafés along this seafront road are currently closed as the promenade is redeveloped. Keep on the lookout for completion dates to see when this drinking district is set to return.

Restaurant du Port ££ Good, licensed, fish restaurant. ⓐ Port du Jadida
ⓣ 023 34 25 79 ⓛ Hours vary; closed Sunday evenings

Restaurant Tchikito ££ A great fish restaurant, with elegant traditional decor in a lively place. ⓐ 4 Rue Mohamed Smiha ⓣ No phone ⓛ Hours vary ⓘ Unlicensed

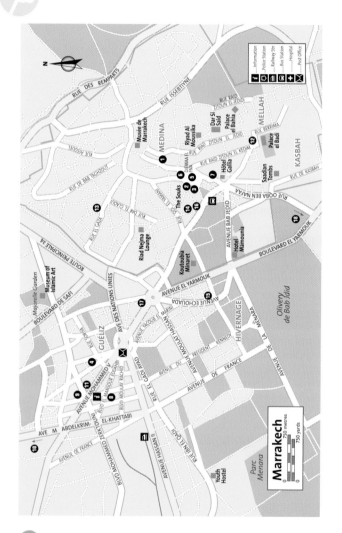

Marrakech

The clash of modern and medieval makes Marrakech the most exotic city in North Africa. This is an exciting and very busy city with a hypnotic charm. Also known as the red city – its medieval walls are made of red mud mixed with lime – it is often called the lifeblood of Morocco. A gateway to the desert and the Atlas Mountains, with firm Berber origins, its modern hotels and infrastructure also cater for the increasing tourist traffic as the city becomes more accessible. With few monuments and sights, it is the city's vibrant culture that is the main draw.

THINGS TO SEE & DO

Ballooning

Try a balloon trip from the suburbs, over the city and into the desert, with **Ciel d'Afrique**.
ⓐ BP 7333 Sidi Abbad ❶ 044 43 28 43 Ⓦ www.cieldafrique.net
🕓 Summer only ❶ Note that most flights are in the early morning, and pre-booking is essential

Djemaa el Fna

Contrary to its translated name, the 'Assembly Place of the Dead' is one of the most alive places on the planet, and a visit to this central square, the heartbeat of Marrakech, is an experience you will never forget. Ordinary and pretty drab in the heat of the middle of the day, there is little to see, apart from a few juice stands and nut sellers. But, it all changes at night, when a myriad of foodstalls appear at sunset and the square transforms into Morocco's nightly carnival, full of exotic sights, sounds and smells. Hypnotic Moroccan music and dancing, snake-charmers, fortune-tellers, acrobats and colourfully clothed water sellers fill the air with their gesticulations and shouts. This is one of Morocco's best offerings and is an unforgettable nightly spectacle – all for free. Choose one of the cafés overlooking the square for a more relaxed view of the feverish activity below. Be particularly wary of pickpockets here, and leave your most valuable belongings in the hotel. Look out for the whirling *sufi gnaoua* dancers, who were originally used to banish evil spirits, and those who peddle sets of second-hand teeth.

Fantasia

You are in for a treat if you are in Marrakech in June when the **Festival of Folklore** is on. Held in the **Palace el Badi** (see page 53), it features Berber music, dance and special fantasia spectaculars. Horsemen charge on steeds, shoot off their guns and perform acrobatics (**❶** 044 44 81 87; ask the tourist office for details). If the festival isn't on, **Chez Ali** hosts a nightly fantasia, with meal included.
ⓐ Safi Road outside Marrakech

Gardens

Marrakech is a pleasant garden city with lots of greenery. **Agdal Gardens** is a vast royal pleasure gardens. Its major attractions are a bit far out, however, so it is best to catch a taxi or hire a bicycle.
ⓐ Just south of the Mellah, or Jewish quarter, and the Royal Palace; enter via the Mechouar, or parade ground **❶** Opening times are very erratic; your best chance is at the weekends. Closed when the King is in residence at the Royal Gardens **❶** Admission free

  Majorelle Garden, a delightful botanical garden once owned by Yves Saint Laurent and originally created by French artist Louis Majorelle, is an oasis of calm, with flourishing bamboo, palms and cacti, and a brightly coloured small art museum.
ⓐ Avenue Yacoub el Mansour in the Ville Nouvelle **❶** 08.00–17.30
❶ Admission charge

  Parc Menara is a popular picnic spot, with its olive and lemon groves. The green-tiled Menzeh pavilion is picture perfect, with the dramatic Toubkal Mountains in the background.
ⓐ From Bab Djedid, take the Avenue de Menara **❶** 05.00–18.30
❶ Admission free

○ Food stalls surround the lively square of Djemaa el Fna at night

Horse-drawn carriage tour

Locally called *calèches*, these are Marrakech's most romantic way to travel. Try a tour of the red-walled ramparts of the city at sunset or of the Circuit de La Palmeriae, which has over 150,000 palm trees. Negotiate a price before you embark.

ⓐ Place Foucault, and at some hotels

Hotel Mamounia

Buy a mint tea and you can access the gardens of Marrakech's most luxurious hotel, the favourite of Winston Churchill. It is still frequented by the Hollywood set and their ilk. The elegant gardens are a mix of European and Moroccan design. At time of press the hotel was at the tail-end of a massive renovation. The reopening date is set for early 2008 but subject to change.

ⓐ Hotel Mamounia, Avenue Bab Djedid ⓣ 044 44 44 09
ⓦ www.mamounia.com

⬥ *Carpets for sale at Souk Zrabia*

Koutoubia Minaret

The Koutoubia Minaret is the spiritual guardian of Marrakech and one of the most elegant minarets in the Islamic world. Each of its four sides is designed differently, which was revolutionary at the time of its construction towards the end of the 12th century. Silhouetted against the setting sun, it provides the backdrop from the transformation of the Djemaa el Fna. The exterior is floodlit at night.
❶ Entry is for Muslims only

Musée de Marrakech

Built in 1997, this museum tells the history of the city in the confines of a restored early 20th-century home once owned by a minor noble. While the displays are of interest, including a number of old photos chronicling the city as it once looked, it's the house itself that truly captivates.
ⓐ Place ben Youssef ❶ 024 39 09 11 ❶ 09.00–18.30

Palace el Badi

The cool and lavish home of the Festival of Folklore in June (see Fantasia, page 50), this palace is a great place to visit in the middle of the day when you need to escape from the heat.
ⓐ Beside the Royal Palace on Place des Ferblantiers ❶ No phone
❶ 08.30–11.45 & 14.30–17.45 ❶ Admission charge

Palace el Bahia

A visit to this beautiful 19th-century palace is very enjoyable.
ⓐ From Place des Ferblantiers, take Rue Riad Zitoun el-Jdid
❶ 09.00–11.45 & 14.30–17.45

Saadian Tombs

This site, one of the most visited in Morocco, has over 100 mosaic-decorated tombs. Sultan Ahmed El Mansour, the Golden One, is buried in this small graveyard in a beautiful garden setting.
ⓐ Beside the Kasbah Mosque near Bab Agnaou on Rue de la Kasbah
❶ No phone ❶ 08.30–11.45 & 14.30–17.45 ❶ Admission charge

The souks

A wander through the souks of Marrakech is like a step back in time. There are individual markets for wool, leather, slipper makers, blacksmiths as well as olive and apothecary stalls. The maze of small narrow streets can be confusing at first, and is busiest in the early morning or the late afternoon. To get your bearings, it might be wise to hire a guide – the tourist office or your holiday representative will be the best ones to ask about this.

Souk Zrabia (ⓐ Off Rahba Kedima, in a smaller square), where they now sell carpets, was a former slave market until 1912, and is particularly lively.

TAKING A BREAK

Marrakech is one of North Africa's top places to eat. There is a choice of restaurants to suit every palate and wallet. From dining in a palace restaurant to eating at one of the night stalls at Djemaa el Fna, whatever you choose to eat is guaranteed to be a veritable feast for the senses.

Café des Epices £ ❶ Finally a place for a snack and some soul-soothing in the souks. Until this place opened, the chance of a Coca-Cola® anywhere in the maze of shops was impossible. Rejoice! ⓐ 75 Rahba Lakdima ❶ 024 39 17 70 ⏰ 08.00–20.00

Café Glacier and Café de France £ ❷ and ❸ Café Glacier offers a great view of the streets below, whereas Café de France is more crowded and has less of a view. ⓐ Djemaa el Fna ⏰ 06.00–23.00

Café du Livre £ ❹ Local anglos call this bookstore/café home away from home. Stock up on literature and lunch or just sip on some seriously strong coffee. The breakfasts come highly recommended. ⓐ 44 Rue Tarek Ibn Ziad ❶ 024 43 21 49 ⏰ 09.30–21.00 Mon–Sat

Djemaa el Fna £ ❺ There are a number of food stalls in the Djemaa el Fna, and nothing can compare with the taste of a grilled meal eaten on a

wooden bench in the heart of the square. Don't eat here if you have a
delicate stomach and are not used to spicy food.

Pâtisserie de Princes £ ❻ Pastries to make you feel like royalty.
ⓐ 32 Rue de Bab Agnaou ❶ 024 44 30 33 ⏰ 05.00–23.30

Argana Restaurant ££ ❼ Good Moroccan fare and a great view. Tajines
and salads at an affordable price. ⓐ 1 Place Djemaa el Fna
❶ 024 44 53 50 ⏰ 05.00–23.00 ❶ Cash only

Al Fassia £££ ❽ Traditional Moroccan cuisine focusing on Fassi cuisine
(dishes from Fès). A choice of lamb tajines to tempt your palate.
ⓐ 55 Boulevard Zerktouni ❶ 024 43 40 60 ⏰ 12.00–14.30 & 19.30–23.00
❶ Accepts major credit cards

Bagatelle Restaurant £££ ❾ Good-value French restaurant. ⓐ 101 Rue
de Yougoslavie ❶ 024 43 02 74 ⏰ 12.00–14.00 & 19.00–23.00 Thur–Tues

Kosybar £££ ❿ More than just a bar, this funky eatery boasts one of
the best wine cellars in the country. Great food adds to the fun.
ⓐ 47 Place des Ferblantiers ❶ 024 38 03 24 ⏰ 12.00–23.00

Le Jacaranda £££ ⓫ Classy French restaurant with excellent service
and a chic European menu. This is one for splurging on, especially for
fans of fondue, which is a bit of a house speciality, or for *foie gras*.
ⓐ 32 Boulevard Zerktouni ❶ 024 44 72 15 ⏰ 12.00–15.00 & 18.30–23.00
ⓦ www.lejacaranda.ma

Le Tobsil £££ ⓬ An intimate place, with excellent food. ⓐ 22 Derb
Abdallah ben Hezzaien, near Bab Nkob (Nkob Gate) ❶ 024 44 40 52
⏰ 19.30–23.00 Wed–Mon

Nikki Beach £££ ⓭ If you're staying somewhere without a pool,
then this collection of eateries and swimming pools is the place to go –

especially if you have kids. Make sure to bring your bathing suit! **a** Royal
Golf Palace, Circuit de la Palmeraie **t** 024 36 87 27 **l** 10.30–19.00

Restaurant Yacout £££ **14** The best restaurant in town, with exquisite
local cuisine. Worth a splurge for those who push the boat out when on
holiday. Enjoy an aperitif on the rooftop terrace. **a** 79 Sidi Ahmed Soussi
t 024 38 29 29 **w** www.yacoutmarrakech.com **l** 19.00–01.00 Tues–Sun
! Licensed; book in advance

AFTER DARK

Comptoir **15** P. Diddy (formerly Puff Daddy) booked this entire bar for
his 33rd birthday, flying in models and actors to join the fun – but those
days are over. The interiors are still beautiful, but the chic set have long
since left. Still, it's a nice place to enjoy a drink even if it's no longer the
hippest place in town. **a** Avenue Echouada **t** 024 43 77 02
l Mon–Thur 16.00–01.00, Fri & Sat 12.00–01.00

Diamant Noir **16** Feeling daring? This club is avoided by the glitterati,
yet is all the better for it. Electro meets Arabia at this down-and-dirty
establishment popular with both the local gay community and
bohemian student set. **a** Hotel Marrakech, Place de la Liberté,
Avenue Mohammed V **t** 024 43 43 51 **l** 22.00–04.00

Pacha **17** The élite of the city join visiting models and celebrities at
this massive dance complex located 7 km (4½ miles) south of the city.
Built to resemble a period fort or palace, it is chock-full of courtyards,
restaurants and private nooks to provide a touch of intimacy to the
grand surroundings. Internationally renowned DJs are often booked.
a Boulevard Mohammed VI **t** 061 10 28 87 **l** 23.30–06.30

Piano Bar **18** This piano bar is the place to go if you want a quiet night.
The quality of the playing varies wildly day to day. **a** Hotel les Jardins de
la Koutoubia, 26 Rue de la Koutoubia **t** 024 38 88 00 **l** 17.00–24.00

Ouarzazate

Once a remote and quiet Berber backwater, Ouarzazate is Morocco's gateway to the Sahara Desert, and makes an excellent stopover or base for trips into the sand dunes. It has a distinctly Foreign Legion feel – the French built a garrison town here in the 1920s – and, thanks to its use as a location in the movie industry, it has become a considerable tourist attraction, with a boom in the construction of modern luxury hotels. As with any desert region, it can get very cold, particularly at night, so wrap up warm out of season.

THINGS TO SEE & DO

Atlas film studios

The hit films *Gladiator*, *Lawrence of Arabia* and Oliver Stone's *Alexander* were filmed here. You can tour the sets of the Tibetan monastery used in *Kundun* and some Egyptian sets used in the filming of movies and documentaries about the gorgeous Cleopatra.

● *The famous Atlas Studios are a must for visitors*

ⓐ 6 km (4 miles) west of Ouarzazate, on the Marrakech Road; use a taxi to get out there ⓣ 024 88 21 66 ⓦ www.atlasstudios.com
ⓛ 08.00–18.00; closed if filming a movie, but you might get a job as an extra ❶ Admission charge for tours

Ensemble Artisanal

This is the place to go for stonework carvings, woollen carpets and ceramics made by the local Berbers. It is one of the best artisan workshops in the country, with competitive prices.
ⓐ Avenue Mohammed V, in front of the Kasbah ⓣ 024 88 24 92
ⓛ 09.00–12.00 & 14.30–18.00

Kasbah Tifoultoute

A dramatic kasbah on the banks of the River Tifoultoute. You can eat here in splendid grandeur from a reasonably priced fixed menu. Performances of music and dance often accompany the meal.
ⓐ About 10 km (6 miles) west of Ouarzazate ⓛ 08.00–19.00 Mar–Sept
❶ Admission charge

Quad bikes and mountain bikes

To hire mountain bikes, try **Daya Travels** (ⓐ near Place Mohammed V
ⓣ 024 88 77 07) or **Ksour Voyages** (ⓐ 11 Place du 3 Mars ⓣ 024 88 28 40).
For quad bike tours, contact **Quad Adventure** (ⓐ 7 km/4½ miles from Ouarzazate on Rue Ait Benhaddou ⓣ 024 88 40 24). Otherwise, try **Wilderness Wheels**, which also runs trips into the desert (ⓐ Avenue Mohammed V ⓣ 024 88 81 28 ⓦ www.wildernesswheels.com).

Taouirt Kasbah

The only major tourist attraction here is the remnants of one of the greatest kasbahs of Morocco, the former fort of the Glaoui Berber dynasty. You can hire a guide to take you round here. Ask at your hotel or the tourist office for an official guide.
ⓐ Avenue Mohammed V, on the eastern edge of town ⓛ 08.00–18.00
❶ Admission charge

TAKING A BREAK

Pâtisserie-Glacier des Habous £ Fresh juices, ice cream, sandwiches – join the rest of the town at this small (yet friendly) establishment.
ⓐ Rue du Marché ❶ No phone ❶ 06.00–22.00

Pizzeria Venezia £ Budget-value pizzas, salads and traditional dishes.
ⓐ Avenue Moulay Rachid ❶ 024 88 24 68 ❶ Hours vary

Chez Dimitri ££ Very popular place for tourists and frequented by the movie set too, this restaurant offers a wide-ranging menu that includes great French and Mediterranean dishes as well as Moroccan fare. Hints of Foreign Legion. ⓐ 22 Avenue Mohammed V, next to Hotel Royal
❶ 024 88 73 46 ❶ Hours vary ❶ Licensed

Restaurant Phoenix ££ Italian pastas dishes up to serve the local film community. Expect filling, yet simple versions of familiar dishes. Vegetarians will appreciate the variety of courses available on the menu.
ⓐ Avenue Mohammed V1 behind L'Hotel de Ville ❶ 024 88 83 13
❶ 12.00–22.00

Le Relais Saint Exupéry £££ If you're going to splurge, do it at this romantic establishment specialising in French and Moroccan dishes. It doesn't feel very African, but the intimacy and good-quality food will quickly make you forget. ⓐ 13 Boulevard Moulay Abdellah ❶ 024 88 77 79
❶ Thur–Tues 12.00–15.00 & 18.30–22.30; closed July

AFTER DARK

Avenue Mohammed V Ouarzazate isn't a very party-hardy town. Most restaurants and bars close early and there are no discos of note to recommend. If you are looking for a bit of fun after the sun sets, join locals by walking along Avenue Mohammed V to see what's going on along the main street.

Essaouira

With the most European in layout of all Moroccan towns, Essaouira is Morocco's most relaxed Atlantic resort. It is a magical place of whitewashed streets with blue doors, wide sandy beaches and a chaotic fishing port, with hundreds of blue boats. The city is famous for its craftsmen who work with local *thuya* wood, a mahogany-like hardwood with a particular aroma. Their wares are on offer in the several long-established woodcarving workshops. In recent years, the town has attracted artists and photographers, as well as windsurfers who consider Essaouira's waves the best in Africa, thanks to the alizee wind in spring and summer. Essaouira is an enchanting, mostly unspoilt resort, with Norfolk Island pines and small offshore islands.

It is remote, however, and quite a trip to get there, with only a small number of weekly flights, run by regional airlines operating from Casablanca to the local airport. From Marrakech or Agadir, it will take three to four hours by car (a little more by bus). Holidays that incorporate two different resorts are becoming increasingly popular and combining Agadir and Essaouira or Marrakech and Essaouira are favoured options, so be sure to ask your tour operator if this interests you.

BEACHES

Essaouira has beaches to the north and south of the town. Unless the famous local wind is up, it is safe for bathing. When the water is calm and the weather is hot, **Plage de Safi** is the best of the selection. Camel rides on the beach are particularly atmospheric as the sun goes down.

THINGS TO SEE & DO

Art galleries
With many painters and sculptors now living in Essaouira – many of them picking up quite an international reputation – it is worth a wander around the art shops and galleries to see if you can pick up a bargain.

⬤ *One of many craft workshops and studios to be found in Essaouira*

> **GOATS IN THE TREES**
> Look out for the goats in the branches of trees! The goats are after the argan nut and scale the trees to get this prized food. The nut is used to make the treasured local **argan oil**. Although you will hear of miracle cures from its use, the greatest value of argan oil is in its culinary use for its tasty, characteristic nutty flavour.

Windsurfing

This is the premier place for windsurfing in North Africa. To hire equipment, contact **Magic Fun Afrika**.
ⓐ Boulevard Mohammed V ❶ 024 47 38 56 Ⓦ www.magicfunafrika.com
🕒 09.00–18.00 Mar–Dec

Wood workshops

Great for souvenir hunting – the workshops under the ramparts are home to some of the finest woodcarving in North Africa.

TAKING A BREAK

Fish Stalls £ Fresh fish, grilled on barbecues by the harbour. Great for fresh fish sandwiches for lunch. ⓐ Down by the harbour

Pâtisserie Driss £ Orange juice, coffee and fresh croissants. Great place to relax after a morning stroll. ⓐ 10 Rue Hajjali ❶ 024 47 57 93
🕒 07.00–22.00

El Minzah ££ Fish and Moroccan specialities on the menu.
ⓐ 3 Avenue Okba Nafia ❶ 024 47 53 08 🕒 Lunch and dinner; hours vary
❶ Accepts major credit cards

Taros ££ Taros is a multi-purpose venue that caters to all moods. If you're looking for a cup of tea and a sedate atmosphere, then stick to the ground floor. The higher you go, the boozier it gets. Nibbles are served on all floors. ⓐ Place Moulay Hussein ⓣ 024 47 64 07 ⓛ 11.00–16.00 & 18.00–24.00 Mon–Sat

Chez Sam £££ A seafood institution perched on the edge of the docks and serving the freshest of produce from the ocean. ⓐ Port de Pêche ⓣ 024 47 62 38 ⓛ 12.00–15.00 & 19.00–22.30 ⓘ Licensed; accepts major credit cards

Dar Loubane £££ Seafood restaurant with fish cooked in Moroccan and French styles. ⓐ 24 Rue de Rif ⓣ 024 47 62 96 ⓛ Lunch and dinner; hours vary ⓘ Accepts major credit cards

Les Alzés Mogador £££ Top local cuisine in a quiet location. ⓐ 26 Rue Skala, beside Hotel Smara ⓣ 024 47 68 19 ⓛ 12.00–15.00 & 19.00–23.00

Les Chandeliers £££ This place offers tasty Moroccan and French cuisine. ⓐ 14 Rue Derb Lallouj ⓣ 024 47 64 50 ⓛ Hours vary

AFTER DARK

Essaouira's options after dark are limited to say the least. If you are looking for something to do, head for the nearest international hotel and find the bar. The **Sofitel Thalasse Mogador** is one of the better choices.

ORSON WELLES AND OTHELLO
Essaouira stars in the Orson Welles classic film version of *Othello*. Welles had very little money and he famously had to borrow table-cloths from the local restaurants to use as costumes during filming. In the town, they have named a square after the director.

RESORTS

Agadir

Agadir was constructed as a modern resort town after a devastating earthquake in 1960. Today, it seems tailor-made for holidaymakers, with all the amenities you could ever want for your package holiday, including a great, relatively unspoilt beach.

Wide new boulevards, parks and a relatively modern Medina have replaced what remained of the old town, which is is clean and modern even if the architecture often leaves much to be desired. It is a gentle introduction to Moroccan life for those who don't want too much of a culture shock.

There are few sights of interest in the town itself, but it is the ideal location if you have come on holiday to enjoy sunshine, the beach and a wide variety of watersports and leisure activities. Ultra-modern, relatively tasteful hotels and apartment blocks line the beach (they are all reassuringly earthquake-proof).

BEACHES

The long sandy beach is the main focus of life in Agadir. Here you can sail, water-ski, scuba-dive, fish, windsurf and ride camels to your heart's content. Or simply soak up the rays – Agadir gets an average 300 days of sunshine a year. The beach is flat and the water fairly shallow with a bit of a current, especially if there is any wind. You must be very careful if you have young children running in and out of the water.

To avoid hassle from beach hawkers, it can be a good option to pay a little extra to camp down at one of the private stretches of beaches. If your hotel backs onto the beachfront, then you're not likely to have to pay. The corniche along the side of the sand is where the vast majority of tourist restaurants and bars are located and is the definitive focal point of the action when the sun goes down. For such a popular beach resort, Agadir may seem surprisingly quiet to some.

THINGS TO SEE & DO

Birdwatching

For those interested in our feathered friends, the Souss Estuary is the place to go. From flamingo to Barbary partridge, there is enough here to keep the average twitcher more than happy.

🅐 You can walk from the beach at Agadir, but your best option is to go via car (either hire car or taxi)

Camel rides

Riding a camel on Agadir beach will be one of the highlights of your holiday. Shop around for the best price and watch out for scam artists.

🅐 The dune area to the south of the main beach area is the place to go

Fish market

As well as being Morocco's major tourist resort, Agadir is also a major fishing port. The local fish market is quite a spectacle, especially if you can get there early in the morning.

🅐 In the harbour area 🕒 06.00–10.00; closed Sun

Football

Impromptu football matches take place on the beach at Agadir, especially on a Sunday. Join in if you feel fit enough.

Golf

There are three excellent courses near Agadir – Agadir Royal Golf, Golf des Dunes and Golf du Soleil – and club hire is available from all of these (see page 101).

Jardim de Olhão

Mock Berber buildings and a museum with old photos.

🅐 Avenue du President Kennedy 🕒 08.00–18.30; closed Mon

❶ Admission free

● *Camel safaris on offer at Agadir Beach*

Kasbah
The best place for a panoramic view of Agadir. It is the only remnant of the old town after the earthquake in 1960. There is not really too much to see, apart from the view and a memorial plaque. On one side of the hill, the Arabic words etched out are '*Allah, Malik, Watan*', which translate into English as 'God, King and country'.
❶ It is a long walk up to the kasbah and a hot hike in the middle of the day, so it is better to take a taxi up and walk down again if you are fit.

Municipal Museum
This museum is a modern construction containing some good Berber jewellery exhibits.
ⓐ Boulevard Mohammed V ❶ 028 82 28 94 ● 10.00–19.00
❶ Admission charge

Souk

The walled market, **Souk el-Had**, at Agadir is arguably the cleanest and most modern of the Moroccan souks. The prices are a bit inflated for the tourist in comparison to other cities, but if you have a nose for a bargain and haggle hard then you won't be disappointed. Most of the action takes place in the morning or in the early evening – it is quiet during the heat of midday. Located in the southern suburbs, you may need to take a taxi from your hotel, especially if you are returning laden with souvenirs. There is a shuttle minibus that leaves for the Medina from some of the larger hotels such as the Agadir Beach Club. Ask the tourist office for details. ● The largest market is on Sun; closed Mon

For those who would rather not haggle, the **Uniprix Supermarket** has a limited selection of souvenirs (you can also buy alcohol here). ⓐ On the corner of Boulevard Hassan II and Avenue Sidi Mohammed

Valley of the Birds

Contains a small aviary and zoo and a children's playground.
ⓐ Avenue du Prince Hértier Sidi Mohammed ❶ 028 82 28 94
● 09.30–12.30 & 14.30–18.30 ❶ Admission charge

Watersports

Agadir is a great spot for watersports and you will be able to hire gear from your hotel or directly on the beachfront. Jet skiing, windsurfing and paragliding are particularly popular activities on Agadir Beach. Tarhazoute just north of Agadir has an international reputation for surfing.

TAKING A BREAK

Agadir has a wide range of restaurants to cater for a considerable number of tourists.

SOS Poulet/SOS Pecheur £ Grilled chicken at Poulet. Fried fish at Pecheur. That's all they offer – perfect if you want something tasty and quick.
ⓐ Avenue du Prince Moulay Abdallah ❶ No phone ● Hours vary

Yacout £ While it's open most of the day, Yacout is most famous for its filling breakfasts. The ice cream offered in the afternoon isn't half bad either. ⓐ Avenue du 29 Fevrier ⓣ No phone ⓛ 06.00–late

Fish stalls ££ For the freshest of fish. Can be a bit overpriced. ⓐ At the entrance to the port

Johara £££ Best restaurant in town. An unforgettable experience, with multiple courses of exquisitely prepared local cuisine, and traditional music at night. ⓐ Boulevard du 20 Août ⓣ 028 84 53 53 ⓛ Lunch and dinner; hours vary ⓘ Licensed; accepts major credit cards

Mimi La Brochette £££ French cuisine with a diverse menu, including fresh fish, brochettes (kebabs) and omelettes. ⓐ Rue la Plage ⓣ 028 84 03 87 ⓛ Hours vary; closed Fri eve & Sat lunch

AFTER DARK

Zanzibar You might be in North Africa, but this popular post-dinner bar is all dressed up to look much more equatorial. Bring a touch of Kenya to your North African adventure – just be sure the alcohol content in the drinks doesn't make you see pink elephants! ⓐ Hotel Riu Tikida Beach, Chemin des Dunes ⓣ 028 84 54 00 ⓛ 19.00–01.00

Nightclub
Papa Gayo Definitely Agadir's most popular nightclub. It thankfully avoids overplaying too much Eurotrash favourites and features an altogether more sophisticated mix of tunes than other Moroccan venues. ⓐ Hotel Riu Tikida Beach, Chemin des Dunes ⓣ 028 84 54 00 ⓛ 22.00–04.00

◗ *Snake-charmer in Marrakech market*

EXCURSIONS
Out & about

The Rif

The Rif has by far the most dramatic and wild scenery in Morocco – the mountains here run parallel to the Mediterranean coast, forming imposing cliffs overlooking small coves with sandy beaches, and cutting off the region from the rest of Morocco and Europe. Once the preserve of the country's fiercest Berber tribes, who have occupied the area since Neolithic times, in years past it has been known as bandit country, and not a place for foreign visitors. The area is also notorious for its cannabis industry, with remnants still around, so you need to take care. But the Rif has changed significantly, with increased policing and a considerable clampdown on drug trafficking. With massive investment, it is becoming an enticing tourist area with fabulous, scenic vistas and secluded beaches. You will still be offered *kif* or hashish anywhere you go, and it is not recommended to indulge. Even though it is theoretically not illegal to smoke, it is illegal to be in possession, and many of the dealers are police informers.

The area's natural barrier also proved a good defence against the Spanish, who, despite this being technically their Protectorate in 1912, fought continual battles – most of them defeats – against the local tribes until 1925. Over the years, Riffians have continued to be independent – they were strongly involved in gaining Moroccan independence in 1956 and soon after, when they felt under-represented by the newly formed national government, they rebelled, albeit unsuccessfully.

The road through the Rif, atop the mountain range itself, is spectacular scenery, especially from Chefchaouen to Al Hoceima.

CHEFCHAOUEN (CHAOUEN)

This gem of northern Morocco is set in a beautiful mountain valley. With whitewashed, Andalucian-style houses and blue doors, it is the most picturesque town in the Rif and worth a day trip in its own right. The small kasbah, which has been recently restored, encloses a tranquil garden and a small museum.

🔺 *Chefchaouen's white houses lie nestled in a remote valley*

Considered a holy city of Islam – the region was a pilgrimage site to the grave of Moulay Abdessalam Ben Mchich, patron saint of the Djebali tribesmen – Christians were not permitted to enter for many years. Until the 1920s, only three Europeans are recorded as having entered the town. It was Moulay Rachid, a follower of the saint, who actually founded the town, using it as a base to launch attacks on European colonialists.

Times have changed, and European tourists are now welcome in this wonderful town which still has more of a village feel. A wander around the craftsmen's workshops in the town souks is a pleasant excursion back in time. The attractive Medina has a cobbled main square, **Place Outa el Hammam**, which is lined with cafés. Although filled with tour buses during the day, the square comes to life with a buzz in the evening.

ⓐ 125 km (78 miles) from Tangier ⓘ Souks on Mon and Thur

OUEZZANE

This relaxed mountain town, laid out in a confusing but charming network of cobblestones, is famous for its olive oil and a dynasty of holy men said to be directly related to the Prophet. It is not a tourist trap and has a good, traditional farmer's market on Thursdays.

KETAMA

A place to be avoided, due to its dangerous connection to marijuana smuggling. The trade is controlled by gangs, and the town, a rather dull village surrounded by pine trees, is quite heavily policed.

AL HOCEIMA

This small fishing port has an attractive town beach and a backdrop of olive groves in the surrounding hills. It is popular with tourists who come over the border from Melilla (see page 73). Only a few kilometres away, Asfia has another attractive beach, while just offshore is the attractive, Spanish-owned island of El Penon de Alhuceimas.

ⓐ 330 km (205 miles) from Tangier

Spanish Morocco

There are still two Spanish enclaves in Morocco, and they remain little pockets of Europe on the continent of Africa. The two towns are duty free, and use the euro as currency. It is not possible to take a car hired in Morocco into Ceuta or Melilla, and both tend to be of more interest as political anomalies rather than for their tourist appeal.

CEUTA (SEBTA)

A Spanish enclave since 1640, there is admittedly little to see in Ceuta, aside from some well-preserved colonial architecture. The city is mostly a military base, and has been autonomous since 1995. For those in transit from Spain, the ferry crossings at weekends and on Spanish holidays are particularly crowded and can lead to pandemonium, so it is best to avoid travelling at these times. If you are here to buy duty free, alcohol, petrol and some electronic goods are cheaper, but otherwise, goods are expensive compared with Morocco. Since Spain joined the European Union, there have been growing issues with drug trafficking and illegal immigration at the borders.

There are a few diversions, however. **Parque Marítimo** is a quirky aqua park designed by a Catalan architect. There is also a **casino** in the complex and there are good views of Gibraltar if you climb Mount Acho.

MELILLA

Smaller than Ceuta, Melilla's peculiar location, surrounded on three sides by Morocco, makes it an altogether more interesting place, with a stronger Moroccan influence. The old town walls are the major tourist attraction, and there is a substantial amount of modernist architecture to take in, including several art deco and modernist buildings. Thanks to subsidies from Europe, as well as the trade from dealing in contraband, this is a wealthy place by Moroccan standards. There have been strained relationships between the Rif Berber and Spanish communities in the past, but this appears to be changing rapidly, and the town is now known for being quite friendly.

Larache & Lixus

Most visitors to the former Spanish port of Larache come to see the Roman ruins at Lixus, but this town is also a pleasant stopover, with a nice beach, kasbah and colonial architecture.

A day trip to Larache and the ruins at Lixus can be made from Tangier, which is 85 km (53 miles) from the town, but it is easier if you are based in Asilah, only 40 km (25 miles) away. Travelling by shared taxi or by hire car is recommended.

LARACHE

There is a really fine beach here, just to the north of town, across the estuary. To get there, take a small ferry boat that leaves from near the harbour or catch bus no. 4. The kasbah in Larache, called the Stork's Castle, contains a very impressive 17th-century colonial fortress. Now used as a music school, the fortress is not open to the public. For shoppers, the small Medina is also worth checking out for bargains.
ⓐ Enter by Bab el Khemis

LIXUS

These Roman ruins are the site of the legendary 'Garden of Hesperides', where Hercules picked golden apples after slaying a local dragon (see page 25 for further details).
🕐 Sunrise to sunset ❶ Admission charge

🔺 *Roman ruins at Lixus*

Volubilis & Moulay Idriss

The Roman ruins at Volubilis and the sacred town of Moulay Idriss can be reached easily from Fès and Meknès. A relaxed full day trip from Meknès could include both of these sights.

VOLUBILIS

A great place filled with acres of evocative Roman ruins, these are the best in Morocco, and set in beautiful mountain scenery. The former capital of the Roman province Mauretania Tingitana, Volubilis was founded by Juba II, a descendant of Hannibal who married Cleopatra's daughter. Highlights here include the Triumphal Arch and some extraordinarily well-preserved mosaics. Look out for the House of Orpheus, Poseidon on a seahorse and Diana and her nymphs in the House of Venus.

ⓐ 30 km (19 miles) from Meknes, 70 km (43½ miles) from Fès ⓛ Sunrise to sunset ❶ Admission charge

⬤ *The Triumphal Arch at Volubilis is well-preserved*

MOULAY IDRISS

One of the most important places for Moroccan Muslims, this town is where Moulay Idriss, town namesake and the creator of the country's first great Arab dynasty, is buried. Not only was he Morocco's greatest saint, he was a relative of the Prophet and managed to convert most of Morocco's Berber community to Islam. Needless to say, the town is a popular place for pilgrimages – a large religious festival is held here in his honour each September, and the largest *moussem*, or saint's festival, is also held here each year, around May, bringing Moroccan Berbers from all over the country. Non-Muslims can visit the *moussem* during the day but are not permitted to stay overnight during the festival.

Be aware that most of the major attractions in Moulay Idriss are religious shrines and therefore not open to non-Muslims. Nonetheless, it is a pleasant town to wander around. Climb up through the narrow windy streets to get a view of the green roofs of the shrines.

ⓐ About 4 km (2½ miles) from Volubilis

🔺 *Moulay Idriss is a place of pilgrimage for Muslims*

Middle Atlas

The Middle Atlas Mountains are limestone escarpments with wonderful cedar forests and a network of small Berber market towns with ruined kasbahs. The French arrived here in colonial times and made many of the towns into hill stations and ski resorts, with Swiss-type chalets replacing the traditional architecture.

From Meknès or Fès you can take day trips into the Middle Atlas to see the towns of the twin valleys of Ifrane or Sefrou, or head to the East to see Taza. These towns can also be used as starting routes for a more extensive journey into the remote, eastern part of Morocco and the Sahara, via a scenic route south to the city of Marrakech.

IFRANE VALLEY

The Ifrane is the more attractive of the two valleys south of Fès, with a chain of lakes and pretty Berber towns. Perched on a hilltop at the start of the Middle Atlas mountain plateau, **Immouzer-Kandar** is a popular summer destination to escape the stifling heat of Fès. The ancient kasbah is in ruins and the dominant architecture in the town is French colonial. A three-day apple festival is held here in August, and there is a small souk on Mondays.

ⓐ 36 km (22 miles) south of Fès

LAKE ROUTE

This route, its turnoff just beyond Imouzzer-Kandar, takes you through a landscape featuring a chain of pretty lakes. Lake Dayou is the best and most popular of these, with diverse birdlife to view and row boats to hire. The **Chalet du Lac** is quirky and an excellent place to grab a spot of lunch by the water.

ⓐ Lake Dayou (Dayet Ayou) is 9 km (5½ miles) south of Imouzzer-Kandar, just off the N8 road

IFRANE

This former French colonial hill town is now a bourgeois ski resort filled with chalets and a royal palace – a kind of yellow, Gothic chateau – hidden in the hills. It is also the home to the new, large Al Akhawayn University. There is not a tremendous amount to see here, and it is expensive. For skiing, you need to go to nearby Mischliffen. Ask your holiday representative, hotel or the tourist office for details.

ⓐ 60 km (37 miles) from Fès

AZROU

This is a typical Middle Atlas Berber town, with a mountain backdrop and houses with red or green pitched tiled roofs. It is also a centre for local wood crafts and there is a carpet and weaving cooperative in town. The **Ensemble Artisanal** is under the large rocky outcrop, or *azrou*, that gave the town its name. Prices are fixed, which is good for shoppers who don't wish to haggle. Just to the south of Azrou are some cedar forests with large colonies of Barbary monkeys. Although they have been traditionally called apes because of their short tail, this is incorrect and they are actually macaque monkeys.

ⓐ 60 km (37 miles) south of Meknès ❶ Souk on Tues

KHENIFRA

A large garrison town with few sights. It does, though, have dark red buildings with green doors, and a traditional souk where few tourists venture.

ⓐ 82 km (51 miles) south of Azrou ❶ Souks on Wed and Sun

SEFROU VALLEY

The alternate route south, along the Sefrou Valley, is more desolate. In the foothills of the mountains, **Sefrou** is an attractive small town, 28 km (17 miles) south of Fès, with an ancient Medina and ochre walls as well as an extensive Mellah, or Jewish quarter. A cherry festival is held in late June here each year, with folklore dances central to celebration.

❶ Souk on Thur

TAZA

On the route from Fès to remotest eastern Morocco, this is an ancient fortress town which separates the Rif and Middle Atlas Mountains. The old town hangs on a cliff above the newer town. The **Taza Gap** is the only natural pass between the Eastern Rif and the rest of Morocco. Taza's magician, Bou Hamra, was its most infamous son and a real confidence trickster who claimed he could speak to corpses, among other miracles. Eventually caught, he was thrown to the lions, which famously refused to eat him.

ⓐ 120 km (75 miles) from Fès

MIDELT

This one-street market town, the gateway to the Ziz Valley, is rather drab if not for its dramatic location. To see its famous carpets, find the old souk, or Souk Djedid, where colourful, local, geometric-patterned products are slung outside for natural bleaching. A classic four-wheel drive circuit takes place near Midelt. Known as the Cirque Jaffar, it takes half a day to drive around.

ⓐ 210 km (130 miles) south of Fès; market is behind the bus station

❶ Large souk on Sun

🔺 *Berber women and children from Midelt*

Ziz Valley & Tafilalt Oasis

The Ziz Valley, which skirts the Algerian border, is a long way from most resort towns. Yet the great oasis of Tafilalt and the sand dunes of Erg Chebbi make it one of Morocco's most memorable regions. Hardy travellers can head out for a few days here into a land filled with the ghosts of the Foreign Legion and Berber nomadic tribes.

ZIZ VALLEY

Er Rachidia

This former French garrison town has been transformed into a rather modern Moroccan town. Its large student population means there is a good buzz at night – and it is a suitable base for trips into the desert.

ⓐ 360 km (224 miles) from Fès

Erfoud

Erfoud was founded by the French Foreign Legion as a military base to control the Tafilalt Oasis. It makes a good base for excursions further south. A Festival of the Dates is held here in October.

ⓐ 80 km (50 miles) south of Er Rachidia, 290 km (180 miles) north-east of Ouarzazate. ❶ Souk on Sat

TAFILALT OASIS

Merzouga and the Dunes

The Erg Chebbi sand dunes, which rise to 150 metres (almost 500 ft), are a spectacular sight, particularly at sunset. Nearby Merzouga has a handful of hotels and a small lake in the vicinity, where, in the winter, flocks of flamingos make the air bright pink.

ⓐ Merzouga is 57 km (35½ miles) south of Erfoud ❶ Souk on Sat

Rissani

This quiet desert town only really comes to life on market days, when donkeys and people amass in the small square and the kasbah.

ⓐ 22 km (14 miles) south of Erfoud ❶ Souks on Sun, Tues and Thur

Toubkal Massif & Tizi n'Test

This is high mountain territory and will only really be on the itinerary of those who go trekking or who want to take the scenic route between Marrakech and Taroudannt.

TOUBKAL NATIONAL PARK

A trekker's paradise with high wild mountain scenery. Most of the terrain here is inaccessible by road. Nearby **Djebel Toubkal** is the highest mountain in North Africa, at 4,167 metres (13,671 ft).

TIZI-N'TEST

This is certainly the most scenic road in Morocco and cuts a swathe through the mountains that link Marrakech to Taroudannt. It is over 200 km (124 miles) of twisting, windy road – driving it is not for the faint-hearted.

OUIRGANE

A small village that is used as a base for hiking by hardy trekkers and climbers who plan an assault on the peak of Djebel Toubkal (see above).

TIN MAL MOSQUE

This is one of the few mosques in Morocco open to non-Muslims. It has a spectacular location above a river valley, although it is under renovation. ◕ Most days, but may be closed Fri, as it is still used by the local villagers

TIZI N'TEST PASS

This high mountain pass, 2,100 metres (6,890 ft) above sea level, is a hair-raising ride with sheer cliffs suddenly before you as you twist around narrow corners. There is a viewing point at a TV tower, with the best panoramic vistas. As you descend rapidly into the valley, the views get even more spectacular – you will breathe a sigh of relief when you reach level ground again.

Ourika Valley & Oukaïmeden

OURIKA VALLEY

This popular day trip up the mountains will provide respite from the stifling heat of Marrakech in the middle of summer. Charter a *grand taxi* for the day or hire a car for a journey that takes you through incredible scenery, along a valley cut into the High Atlas Mountains. Shoppers might want to visit some of the small pottery shops on the side of the road.

The Valley

The start of the Ourika Valley is at Tnine de L'Ourika, with a very good local farmer's market souk on Mondays. Get there early if you can, as

🔺 *Oukaïmeden panoramic mountain map*

it can get pretty crowded out with tour buses towards mid-morning. A little further on the road is Dar Caid Ouriki, with an old kasbah that is unfortunately in ruins, albeit in a dramatic location. There is a curious and unusual brick mosque at Arhbalou.

Setti Fatma

This village is dramatically situated on the banks of a river, with steep sides rising up into the mountains. A series of seven waterfalls are within a short hike, the first about 20 minutes' walk from the town, with a cool, clear bathing pool. Look out for cheeky Barbary monkeys in the walnut trees. The waterfalls are very popular at the weekend, when the area becomes inundated with young Moroccan daytrippers. A moussem, one of the most important religious festivals in Morocco, takes place here in August, but it is also the time of a great rural market. You can hike out to a *koubba*, or saint's tomb, around which the moussem takes place.

🚌 67 km (42 miles) from Marrakech ❶ Non-muslims are not permitted to enter the green-roofed shrine.

OUKAÏMEDEN

The views on the route to Oukaïmeden from Arhbalou are spectacular on a clear day. The road climbs dramatically up a series of steep twists and turns, and hamlets of small Berber dwellings hug the hills.

Ouka, as it is known, is Morocco's number-one winter holiday destination, with fairly nondescript skiing chalets and a few hotels, and good piste and off-piste skiing between late December and late March. Conditions are best mid-January to mid-February and equipment is available to hire. In summer, it makes a good starting point for a series of hikes into the mountains. If you hire a local guide, you can hike out to see prehistoric rock carvings, unique to Africa, but very similar to ones found in northern Europe. A map in the Club Alpine hut in the town will show you where they are if you want to venture out alone.

Before you head back, continue up the road past the resort, to the TV station aerial. Weather permitting of course, it is a spectacular view.

🚌 75 km (47 miles) from Marrakech

Aït Benhaddou, Dadès Valley & Tinerhir

AÏT BENHADDOU

On the edge of a palm oasis, this collection of kasbahs is one of the most impressive in the south of Morocco. It is one of the most-visited tourist spots, familiar from being featured in many films, including *Gladiator*, *Jesus of Nazareth* and *Lawrence of Arabia*. It can get busy in the middle of the day with tour buses, so come early if you want to experience the magic of the place at a more exclusive and less frantic pace.

ⓐ 32 km (20 miles) north of Ouarzazate

DADÈS VALLEY

This is the valley of one-thousand kasbahs. It is a broader valley than its sister Drâa Valley (see page 87) to the south of Ouarzazate. Many of the kasbahs are in a ruinous state, but they are evocative of a time past.

Skoura

The Skoura oasis appears suddenly from the barren landscape, marking the entrance to the Dadès Valley. The first kasbah – the 17th-century kasbah of Amerhidl – is 500 m (547 yds) to the left of the road, before Skoura village. From Skoura, a maze of paths crisscrosses the oasis, lined with irrigation canals leading to ochre kasbahs.

ⓐ 42 km (26 miles) north-east of Ouarzazate ❶ Souk on Mon and Thur

Dadès Gorge

This gorge, translated as 'sabre cut', is a steep incision into the mountains. It is a spectacular drive through it, from the moment you turn off at Boumalne. The gorge is wide at first, as you pass a ruined kasbah, with almond and poplar trees framing the route. The road then gets narrower as the steep, rocky incline on either side is transformed into strange, towering spires. At Aït Arbi, a spectacular cluster of kasbahs stands at the foot of an enormous rocky promontory, known as 'the brain of the Atlas'. Further on at Tamnalt, the strange rock formations dubbed the 'hills of the human bodies' have foot-like protrusions jutting

🔺 *Aït Benhaddou kasbahs on the edge of an oasis*

from the cliffside. At Aït Oudinar, a track leads round to the Todra Gorge, accessible only by four-wheel drive.

📍 116 km (72 miles) north-east of Ouarzazate

TINERHIR

This former garrison town for the Foreign Legion is suitable for a stopover, with a cluster of restaurants, a large oasis and a good kasbah.

📍 169 km (105 miles) east of Ouarzazate ❗ Souk on Tues

Todra Gorge

This is perhaps the most spectacular gorge in Morocco, but it is only accessible with four-wheel drive or by hiking. In some places, the cliffs are about 300 m (984 ft) high. It is a favourite for rock climbers.

📍 181 km (112½ miles) north-east of Ouarzazate

◆ *Fortified village near Ouarzazate*

Drâa Valley

This ancient caravan trail takes you through desert palm oases and past decaying kasbahs. The fertile valley contrasts with the surrounding bare rock of the semi-desert that is baked by a permanently harsh desert sun. Despite being Morocco's longest river, the Drâa only flows to its potential after heavy rain. Legend has it that this valley was once home to crocodiles – local myth claims that the last one was shot in the 1950s.

In the valley, the people live in fortified *ksour*, or villages, made from the compacted surrounding earth. Built to protect the inhabitants from raids by nomads, these red earthern mud constructions have been moulded into wonderful architectural shapes. The ksour tend to be on the edge of an oasis of palm groves. A network of irrigation channels is used to make best use of the meagre quantities of water in the area. Try the delicious, local boufeggous dates, which are justly famous. It is a 328 km (204 mile) round trip between Ouarzazate to Zagora. An alternative is to stay overnight in Zagora and take a trip further south to Tamegroute and the dunes at Tinfou.

TIZI-N-TINIFIFFT PASS

After 40 km (25 miles) the road to Zagora starts to climb dramatically. The top of this 1,660 m (1,815 yds) pass holds incredible views of the surrounding mountain peaks.

AGDZ

A rather drab administrative centre with a kasbah sitting on the hill to the east, this town's saving grace is its carpets. On Thursdays, the souk comes alive with brightly coloured carpets, draped in their hundreds over the walls of the red *pisé* (built of sun-baked earth) houses. A kasbah sits on the hill to the east.
ⓐ 68 km (42 miles) from Ouarzazate

TAMNOULGALT & TIMIDERTE

The crenellated ksour houses at Tamnougalt, once the capital of the region, are the most impressive in the Drâa Valley. Some of the buildings

87

here are still inhabited by Berbers. The kasbah at Timiderte is iconic and isolated in a sea of grey-coloured rock.

TINZOULINE

This is the largest ksour in the middle Drâa region, with a dramatic setting surrounded by stunning mountain scenery. The Monday souk is especially lively.

ⓐ On the main road between Agdz and Zagora

ZAGORA

The great stony *hammada* (desert) that leads to the Sahara proper starts at this dusty, desert frontier town. If you are so inclined, Zagora is a good place from which to organise a long camel trek into the desert. For the less adventurous, Zagora's *jebel* (black hill) is an old volcano and a great spot from which to watch the sunset. Keep an eye out for the town's famous, much-photographed road sign – '52 days to Timbuktu' – by camel, presumably. It wouldn't be possible to do this trip now, as the Algerian border is currently closed. There is a large date palm oasis just south of town at Amazraou – a great, cooling place to walk during the heat of the day.

ⓐ 96 km (60 miles) south-east of Agdz

TAMEGROUTE

This town has been a centre of Islamic learning since the 17th century. It is also a centre for pottery, and a good place to shop for ceramics, particularly its rough, earthenware pots, which have primitive designs, coloured palm-tree green.

ⓐ 18 km (11 miles) from Zagora

TINFOU DUNES

Here begin the dramatic dunes of the Sahara. Tinfou is a great place for a short camel trek off into the sandy beyond.

ⓐ 7 km (4½ miles) from Tamegroute, 25 km (15½ miles) from Zagora

Taroudannt
mountain oasis

About an hour and a half drive from Agadir, Taroudannt is a comfortable day trip from that resort. Taroudannt is spectacularly located, with the snowpeaks of the High Atlas as a backdrop to an attractive town with a walled Medina. It is a setting that befits what was once the capital of a 12th-century Moroccan empire. Orange and olive groves thrive outside the city walls.

RAMPART TOUR

Take a trip around Taroudannt in a horse-drawn *calèche* (carriage) making sure to negotiate the price before setting off. Early morning or late afternoon, when the ochre colour of the walls is most vibrant in the setting sun, is a good time to choose. If the moon is full, it could be the most romantic moment of your holiday.
➋ Palais el Salaam Hotel on Avenue Moulay Ismail

SOUKS

Great for yellow leather *babouches* (slippers), chunky Berber jewellery and other leather goods and Berber handicrafts. The place has an entirely more relaxed feel than most other tourist souks. You will get a better bargain here than in Agadir, especially if you visit on market days.
➋ Around Bab el Khemis (Thursday's Gate) 🕐 Souks on Thur and Sun

TANNERIES

If you don't make it to Fès or Marrakech, then you should check out the Taroudannt version of the traditional Moroccan tannery. Although on a smaller scale than these two cities, the tannery is equally smelly and colourful to boot. No automation here either, as skins are prepared by hand, then cured and dyed in large, coloured vats.
➌ Outside the walls of the town; leave the Medina through Bab Taghount, turn left and look for the signpost on the right

Tafraoute, Tiznit & Goulimine
deep south

TAFRAOUTE–TIZNIT ROUTE

Here, pisé villages nestle in a valley of oases beneath curious, twisted rock formations and barren scenery. Tafraoute, 144 km (90 miles) south-east of Agadir, the relaxed administrative centre of the surrounding villages, has almond trees in full blossom in early spring and a souk held on Wednesdays. Tata, to the south-east, is the main base in this exceptionally beautiful region, while 62 km (39 miles) south, at Akka, lurk some of the most impressive prehistoric rock carvings in North Africa (you will need a local guide to find them).

TIZNIT

Surrounded by pink city walls, Tiznit's central Medina is its most attractive element. Famous for its silver jewellery, the town has a tradition of craftsmanship going back to a time when Jewish artisans formed the majority of the town's inhabitants. There is a very good beach 17 km (11 miles) west of the town at Aglou.

🚌 91 km (57 miles) south of Agadir ❶ Souk on Thur

SIDI-IFNI

A Spanish colony until 1969, now with a thriving port, this town seems curiously out of place, with its art deco buildings and a Catholic church. It is popular with surfers and paragliders.

🚌 165 km (103 miles) south of Agadir ❶ Souk on Sun

GOULIMINE (GUELMIME)

A dusty desert gateway, Goulimine, 199 km (124 miles) south of Agadir, holds a great Saturday camel market, which runs all year, except in the height of summer. It has become slightly touristy, with the Tuareg – the famous 'blue men' of the desert – willing to pose for pictures for a price.

⊙ *Authentic, quality leather Moroccan slippers are a real bargain*

Food & drink

Moroccan cooking is a mix of cuisines from the cultures that have influenced the country through the ages, including tastes from France and Spain as well as Berber and Middle Eastern recipes that have been embellished by the local chefs.

Moroccan food is tasty and exotic but it can be quite spicy. However, the food served in hotels and in restaurants in tourist resorts is usually less so, and fans of hot and spicy food may be better off exploring the restaurants used by the locals. Many of these are of excellent quality, and fairly inexpensive.

The best Moroccan food you can eat will be home prepared. If you are lucky enough to be invited for a family meal in a Moroccan home, then you are in for a treat. Meal time is the great social event of the day in Moroccan homes.

The national dish is couscous (like semolina grains) and each Moroccan cook prepares it in a slightly different way.

At the top end of the market, in the best restaurants, traditional Moroccan or colonial cuisine is served with Western-style efficiency. In many cities, old palaces have been converted into sumptuous

● *Popular food stalls in Marrakech's Djema el Fna square*

atmospheric dining rooms that are an absolute treat to dine in. Small local restaurants offer the same traditional food at lower prices, often in similarly authentic surroundings.

On the street, numerous vendors with makeshift grills serve tender mutton, grilled fish, fresh salads, thick *harira* soup (see page 96) and hunks of bread. You should go easy on your stomach at first, but you will soon adapt to this most Moroccan of culinary feasts.

BREAKFAST

In most tourist hotels there will be a buffet with the usual array of cereals, toast, fruit, juice, coffee and tea. Traditional Moroccan breakfasts, however, are *beghir* (semolina pancakes) or flaky pastries filled with nuts, cinnamon and dried fruits. In rural areas, breakfast fare is more simple, and freshly baked traditional bread dipped in olive oil with a glass of mint tea can be the order of the day. If you are out and about early, there are French pâtisseries in most tourist resorts and city centres, so you can always replenish your energies with a coffee and croissant.

❶ Many Moroccan restaurants are unlicensed, but in most tourist areas you will be able to find a licensed restaurant if you look about. During Ramadan, however, be aware that even these restaurants will not serve alcohol in the middle of the day. Some Moroccan restaurants do not accept credit cards, so you need to be wary of this and carry some cash. In the tourist areas, restaurants are more likely to accept credit cards.

LUNCH/SNACKS

Lunch and snacks usually consist of *brochettes* (like kebabs), *briouats* (stuffed pittas), *pastilles* (pastry parcels), kebabs or spicy sausages, all sold at hawkers' stalls. *Harira* stews and snails are also available at stalls.

STARTERS

In a Moroccan restaurant, this is likely to be a salad. *Salade marocaine* is the most common and will contain diced vegetables (peppers, tomatoes and beetroot) and potato. Tuna salad is also on most menus.

MAIN COURSES

The dish that will feature on every restaurant menu is couscous, which at its best when fluffy and light. On its own it is pretty bland, but as a complement to spicy lamb, chicken or fish and vegetables, it is delicious. It can be cooked in hundreds of ways and you are unlikely to taste the same recipe twice. As well as couscous, there are plenty of other choices on restaurant menus, and in the resorts you will get a wide variety of familiar dishes, from fish – such as *daurade* (sea bream) or *loup de mer* (sea bass), all cooked very simply – to steaks and pizza. You can also get some really good seafood, with lobster, squid, oysters, shrimps and prawns all gracing the menus of resort restaurants.

Vegetarian

Some of the restaurants in major resorts have started to include veggie options on their menus, and you can often order couscous without meat, though you may still get it in a meat broth in some places. Depending on the type of vegetarian you are, you can get dishes with just cheese and eggs (such as pizzas and omelettes). If you are vegan or don't eat dairy products, then you are going to have problems and a very limited diet, and you may be best to stick to Western-style restaurants.

DESSERTS

Moroccan desserts tend to be very sweet. Some options include *seffa* (sweet couscous) or rice pudding flavoured with nuts, cinnamon, raisins or rosewater. Others are basically a series of honey-soaked sugary pastries filled with dates and nuts. You may find yourself going for some of the very good ice cream or sorbet after a meal if you don't have that sweet a tooth. Diabetics should steer clear of the ultrasweet choices.

DRINKS
Cold drinks

It is recommended that you drink only bottled water during your visit. Most Moroccan restaurants have a range of soft drink options on offer. Freshly prepared juices or pressés are delicious and thirst quenching.

Hot drinks

Coffee- and tea-drinking are part of the social fabric of Morocco and the men can spend hours just chatting over a black coffee and a cigarette. Coffee is served in a range of ways. Served black and strong, like a sweet espresso, is great for those needing a real caffeine injection, although some find it a little bit too sweet and a little gritty. Café au lait (coffee with milk) and cappuccino are very like what you would drink back home in a café. Green tea usually comes with sprigs of mint or with pine nuts or almonds, in a glass. Red tea, which is stewed to death, tastes like poison! Both are really sweet. You are unlikely to get tea with milk unless you are in a Western-style restaurant or upmarket hotel.

Alcoholic drinks

As a Muslim country, alcohol should theoretically be banned in Morocco. But you can get it freely in the major towns and in most restaurants in tourist resort areas. During Ramadan, especially during daylight hours, and on Fridays, it may be more difficult to buy alcohol in some places. Wine, especially red, is produced in Morocco, but the quality is variable. Locally brewed beers include Flag and Stork, and are worth a try.

● *Men can spend hours drinking tea together*

Menu decoder

Most restaurant menus will be printed in French and Arabic.

Beghir A semolina pancake often served with nuts, dried fruits and cinnamon

Briouats Triangular pastry parcels with a savoury filling of minced meat and vegetables

Brochette Grilled meat kebabs, usually of lamb

Cornes de gazelle Cornet-shaped pastry filled with almond paste and honey. Sticky and delicious

Couscous Ground semolina grains – the dietary staple of Moroccans. Traditionally it is served with a thick meat or vegetable stew and cooked in a special, two-tiered pot called a *couscousier*

Harira Hearty, spicy lentil or bean soup often served with large pieces of meat and vegetables

Harissa North African spicy condiment used to accompany *tajines*

Kefta Meatballs, usually lamb, often served in a pocket of bread

Khobz (pain) Traditional Moroccan flatbread considered sacred by locals

Makouda Potato fritters

Mechoui Roasted lamb on a spit or in a special oven, usually served with flat bread

Merguez Spicy sausage

Rayib Moroccan yoghurt

Salade marocaine Local salad with diced vegetables and potato salad

Tajine Hearty stew made most often with lamb, chicken or vegetables

Tanjia A Marrakechi dish of beef or lamb baked in an urn until it is extremely tender

Thé à la menthe Mint tea brewed in a traditional Moroccan teapot

Shopping

Browsing for souvenirs is one of the most enjoyable experiences of a holiday. As with other Arab countries, you need to bargain and this is not everyone's cup of tea. For some people it is great fun, but for others haggling is a hassle. If you don't enjoy it, buy your goods in a shop with a fixed asking price such as Ensemble Artisanal, which is run by the Moroccan government. Bargaining, however, can be a great way to get to know the locals over a free glass or two of mint tea before you buy.

Most of the decorative crafts draw on the themes used in Islamic architecture, which tend to be repetitive, geometric patterns that include floral designs.

CARPETS & RUGS
Moroccan carpets are expensive and generally not as good as those from Iran or Turkey. If you do buy one, don't expect it to be a family heirloom. Check the prices at home and do your homework. Look for hallmarks of quality and shop around for the best price. Do not start to bargain unless you plan to buy. A better buy is a knotted *kilim*, or rug, of Berber origin. The best place to buy these is in the Middle or High Atlas.

GEMSTONES
Semi-precious stones such as amethyst and quartz are for sale in the souks. Be wary of very cheap prices. Similarly, most 'fossils' for sale will be fakes.

HERBS & SPICES
In the souks, spice sellers have the most colourful and fragrant displays. Don't buy spices you can get at home in your local supermarket, as you won't save much. Saffron is the exception and fans of the most luxuriant of spices will save money. Iranian saffron, deep red in colour, is the best. Powdered saffron will be laced with the cheaper cumin powder. Argan oil (see page 62) is another good buy.

JEWELLERY

Moroccan jewellery tends to be tribal and chunky, and though cheap and cheerful, it is not to everyone's taste. Particularly attractive designs include the Hand of Fatima, for good luck, and Tuareg silver crosses.

LEATHER

A wide range of reasonably priced leather goods, from jackets to handbags to belts, are for sale in most souks. The best souvenir is a pair of *babouches* or leather slippers. Those made for men, which can also be worn by women, are soft, flexible and comfortable and come in yellow, grey or white. Those specifically for women are muticoloured and embroidered and not as geared for comfort.

METALWORK

Most of the vast array of metalwork for sale is for the ritual making of tea, including attractive, ornate and decorative trays and the fabulous and very popular silver teapots. Check the joints and that the lid fits properly. Hard to believe they were originally designed in Manchester.

TILES & CERAMICS

Tile-making is a traditional craft, and most often, tiles will be decorated with Islamic designs. Fès and Safi are the two major pottery centres. Geometric blue and white designs are typical of Fès, whereas in Safi they are more ornate and colourful. A popular souvenir is a decorative *tajine* dish. However, practically, the reddish-brown dishes are cheaper and more useful if you plan to make tajines at home. If this is what you are after, head to the Oulja pottery near Salé.

WOODWORK

Some of the finest inlaid wood carving in North Africa comes from the Essaouira workshops below the town's old ramparts (see page 60). Hardwood, from *thuya* trees that grow locally, is used to make ornate chess and backgammon sets and fine sculptures. Buy direct from workshops as wood carvings in the souks of other cities is of inferior quality.

Children

Bringing your children to Morocco will invariably enhance your experience to the country. Moroccan society is firmly based on the family unit and children are greeted with great enthusiasm and affection.

BEACHES & SWIMMING

Children love the beach. A beach full of sand and a bucket and spade will keep most under-tens amused for most of the day. If they get too hot, a dip in the ocean will cool them down nicely. Most older children and teenagers are happy on the beach, too. Most of the beaches are safe for swimming, but you need to be wary of an underwater current at some of the Atlantic beaches. The best beaches for children are found at Agadir (see page 64), Tangier (see page 15), and the Mdiq-Cabo Negro area, where at Marina Smir there is an Aquafun park (see page 22). Aïn Diab in Casablanca offers an alternative at its beach clubs, with excellent swimming pools and other sports facilities (see page 31).

CAMEL & MULE RIDES

Most children love to see camels in the flesh. If they are brave enough, going for a ride on one is a real thrill. They can do this on the beach, as there are special camel trains that pass along resort beaches. Some of the best beach locations to go for these rides include Agadir Beach (see page 64), Tangier and Martel. In the desert, the options for camel rides are best at the dunes of the Sahara. Zagora in the Drâa Valley (see page 88) is the place to go if you want to send your children to Timbuktu, although it is a long way. Also in the Drâa Valley, the Tinfou dunes are a spectacular place for a camel ride.

FILM STUDIOS

A visit to the Atlas film studios in Ouarzazate (see page 57) will provide an impetus to young potential film stars.

GARDENS

Parks and gardens are a great option if you want to use up some of your children's boundless energy. Parc Menara and Majorelle Gardens (see page 50) are the places to go in Marrakech, while the Chellah (see page 28) in Rabat is worth a visit.

HORSE-DRAWN CARRIAGES

Calèche rides are a great way to see the sights, especially if you have kids in tow. Children invariably love the experience. The best places to go for calèche rides are in Marrakech (see page 50) and Taroudannt (see page 89).

NIGHTLIFE

Not the club variety, but just what is happening in the streets. If you are lucky enough to be staying in Marrakech, bring your kids out to Djemaa el Fna (see page 49). It is quite safe and is a fascinating and exotic place to see – especially the snake-charmers and acrobats.

SAFARIS – DESERT & FOREST

The remote dunes in the Drâa Valley (see page 88) at Tinfou and Erfoud are the best places for a desert safari, albeit a bit off the beaten track. Or perhaps you could seek out Barbary monkeys in the forest. The best place to spot them is near Asilah in the cedar forests and the Ourika Valley at Setti Fatma (see page 83).

VISITING OLD RUINS

Depending on their age and interests, some children find visiting ruins boring, but others will have great fun running around pretending to be gladiators. For Roman ruins, visit Volubilis (see page 75), and for the most dramatic kasbahs, you will need to be in the Ouarzazate area (see page 58). The Dadès Valley (see page 84) is also called Valley of the Kasbahs, as it has literally hundreds of them.

Sports & activities

BALLOONING
During the summer, **Ciel d'Afrique** offers balloon trips over Marrakech and into the desert (see page 49).

FISHING
Coarse fishing (permit required) for perch, pike and bass is most popular; there are good lakes near Marrakech and Meknès. There is also beach fishing all along the Atlantic (no permit required). Off the Western Sahara is one of the best places for sports fishing in the world. Try the following:
Best of Morocco For sea fishing ⓐ Seend Park, Seend, Melksham, Wiltshire, SN12 6NZ, UK ⓣ 01380 828533 ⓦ www.morocco-travel.com
Eaux et Forêts For permits ⓐ 11 Rue du Devoir, Rabat ⓣ 037 70 33 25
ⓐ Boulevard Roudani, Casablanca ⓣ 022 27 15 98
Sochatour ⓐ 7 Avenue des Far, Casablanca ⓣ 022 22 75 13
ⓦ www.sochatour.com

GOLF
Morocco is an excellent country for a golf holiday. Try the following:
Agadir Golf du Soleil ⓣ 028 33 73 29, Les Dunes ⓣ 028 83 46 90, Royal Golf d'Agadir ⓣ 028 24 85 51
Casablanca Anfa Royal Golf Club ⓣ 022 36 10 26, Royal Golf Club ⓐ Ben Slimane ⓣ 023 40 07 55
Fès Royal Golf ⓐ Route d'Ifrane ⓣ 055 66 52 10
Marrakech Amelkis ⓣ 024 40 44 14, Palmeraie ⓣ 024 36 87 66, Royal Golf ⓣ 024 40 47 05
Rabat Royal Dar-es-Salam ⓣ 037 75 58 64
Tangier Royal Country Club ⓣ 039 93 89 25

HIKING & CLIMBING
The mountain ranges of Morocco provide excellent hiking possibilities. The High Atlas Mountains, particularly the Imlil and El Kelaa des M'Gouna regions, are the place to go for more experienced cliimbers:

LIFESTYLE

Atlas Tours (Middle Atlas) ⓐ 40 Boulevard Mansour Eddahbi, Marrakech
🕿 024 43 59 77
Club Alpin Français ⓐ Rue Général Henrys, Casablanca 🕿 022 29 72 92
National Association of Guides for the High Mountains (ANGAHM)
ⓐ BP 47, Asni, Marrakech 🕿 024 44 49 79
Ribat Tours (Middle Atlas) ⓐ 6 Rue du Vieux Marrakechis, Guèliz,
Marrakech 🕿 024 43 86 94

HORSE RIDING

Morocco's Arab horses are world famous for their agility and speed.
Cabo Negro ⓐ La Ferma 🕿 039 97 80 75
Fédération Royale de Sports Equestres ⓐ Dar-es-Salam, Rabat
🕿 037 75 44 24
La Roseraie at Ouirgane ⓐ 60 km (36 miles) south of Marrakech
🕿 024 43 91 28

RUNNING

Marrakech marathon is in January. ⓦ www.marathon-marrakech.com

SKIING

Morocco's Middle Atlas region is becoming a cheap ski destination:
Fédération Royale Marocaine de Ski et Montagne ⓐ Parc de la Ligue
Arabe, Casablanca 🕿 022 47 49 79

TENNIS

Agadir, Morocco's tennis capital, has over 130 courts. Most courts are
floodlit for night play, when temperatures are more bearable.

WATERSPORTS

Agadir is the centre of aquatic action, with water-skiing, jet-ski, sub-aqua
diving and even paragliding on the beach. Essaouira is best for top-class
surfing, windsurfing. International windsurf competitions are held here
each spring. Other top surfing venues include Taghazout, near Agadir,
Plage des Nations, at Rabat, and Mehdiya, the beach near Kenitra.

⬥ *Horse riding down the Berber Route*

M'Diq Yachting Club Arranges sailing courses in the summer.
📞 039 97 56 59
Royal Moroccan Sailboat Federation ⓐ Rabat 📞 037 67 09 56
Royal Moroccan Yacht Club ⓐ Rabat 📞 037 72 02 64
Royal Morocco Federation of Surfing and Windsurfing ⓐ Casablanca
📞 022 22 25 90
Yacht Club de Maroc ⓐ Mohammedia 📞 023 32 79 19

Festivals & events

Morocco has several festivals and celebrations throughout the year. However, most of these are religious celebrations based on the lunar-based Islamic calendar – this makes it difficult to predict the exact dates of the festivals, as they change from year to year.

RAMADAN

Morocco's biggest religious festival, Ramadan, lasts for a lunar month and can affect your holiday, so you should be aware of when it falls (usually sometime between late September and late January). There are advantages and disadvantages to visiting Morocco during Ramadan.

All Muslims fast during daylight hours of Ramadan and it can be difficult for holidaymakers to find a place to eat during the day, because many restaurants close. This is especially difficult if you plan on touring the more remote areas of the country outside the tourist resorts. It is a show of utmost respect to the locals not to eat, drink or smoke in a public place during daylight hours. This doesn't mean you shouldn't eat at all, and most hotel restaurants will open up and serve food especially for tourists.

The fast is traditionally broken at sunset with a bowl of *harira* soup (see pages 93 and 96) – if you have fasted, you can pick one up in any of the cafés. The benefit of a visit to Morocco during Ramadan is that during the evenings – and often late into the night – celebrations are in full swing, with music, dancing and celebration in restaurants and cafés.

Ramadan falls on the ninth month of the Islamic calendar (called the *hegira*), the month in which the verses of the Koran were revealed to the Prophet Mohammed. It begins with the night known as *Lailut ul-Qadr* (meaning the Night of Power). The last day of Ramadan is known as *Eid ul-Fitr* (the Festival of the Breaking of the Fast) and this is the biggest festival of them all, with celebrations taking place in most towns and cities.

OTHER NATIONAL HOLIDAYS
Official holidays

1 January	New Year's Day
11 January	Manifesto of Independence
1 May	Labour Day
30 July	Feast of the Throne
14 August	Allegiance of Oued Ed-Dahab
21 August	Youth Day (King's Birthday)
6 November	Green March Anniversary
18 November	Independence Day

These holidays are usually marked by the closure of banks, government offices and many businesses. Many are viewed as family holidays, but there may be processions in the streets.

MOUSSEM & FANTASIA

Moussems (local festivals) are usually in celebration of *marabouts* (local saints) or at harvest time. They are held to gain *baraka* (blessing) from the saint or to give thanks for a successful harvest. Annual pilgrimages are made to the koubba (saint's tomb), accompanied by music and dancing. Some celebrations can last for several days and are quite a spectacle, while others are low-key affairs that may look like a town's ordinary market day.

The largest moussem in Morocco is the **Ben Aissa**, which is held in April/May in Meknès with a large, spectacular fantasia. Also around this time is the **Candle Moussem** in Salé, which features an atmospheric procession with huge lantern candles. The **Moulay Idriss II Moussem** in September involves processions through the streets of Fès. Also in September, the Moulay Idriss Moussem held in Moulay Idriss itself (see page 76) is not really open to non-Muslims, although you can visit during the day.

Fantasia shows are spectacular displays of horsemanship that tend to accompany every Moroccan festival or celebration. They are so popular that they are put on nightly for tourists during the high season in major tourist resorts. Ask the tourist office for details of local events.

FESTIVALS OF MUSIC & CULTURE

Music plays an important part in the life of a Moroccan. Everywhere you go you will hear some kind of music, and there is a variety of Moroccan music festivals in the summer.

May

Festival of Sacred Music in Fès One of Morocco's most interesting and unique cultural events features religious music from around the globe, and runs from late May to June. ⓦ www.fesfestival.com

Gnaoua Music Festival in Essaouira The Gnaoua brotherhoods and their Sufi Islam beliefs have become world famous through their music. The main instruments they use are a kind of African lute and castanets, which beat out a trance-like rhythm. The festival takes place between May and June each year. ⓦ www.festival-gnaoua.co.ma

June

Marrakech Music Festival This is the biggest Moroccan festival, with all kinds of music and spectacle events, including a large fantasia.

Rabat Jazz aux Oudaïas Festival Events for this festival are held in dramatic ruins at Chellah.

August

Asilah's International Festival This festival runs for three to four weeks and features all kinds of different art events, including music, dance and mural painting of the walls about town.

WEDDINGS

Moroccan weddings are like spontaneous festivals. They vary from low-key, small affairs to huge, week-long celebrations as big as a town festival. The Imilchil Marriage Moussem in September is worth checking out, as it is the largest annual collection of Berber marriages. Imilchil is in the High Atlas and the event features dowry negotiations, singing and dancing.

◗ *Donkeys are a standard mode of transport for Moroccans*

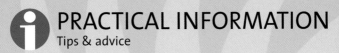

PRACTICAL INFORMATION

Accommodation

Places to stay in Morocco can range from the dirt-cheap to the wildly expensive. Just remember the maxim: you get what you pay for.

Price rating
The ratings in this book are as follows:
£ = up to £50, **££** = £51–£100, **£££** = over £100. All prices are for a single night in a double or twin room.

HOTELS
Casablanca
Hotel du Centre £ Across the street from the Mansour is this budget property that costs just a fraction of the price. Same central location, few frills. ⓐ 1 Rue Sidi Balyout ⓣ 022 44 61 80

Essaouira
Beau Rivage £ There are 21 rooms in total, including six suites at this property right on the Medina's main square. ⓐ 14 Place Moulay Hassan ⓣ 024 47 59 25 ⓦ www.essaouiranet.com/beaurivage

Fès
Hotel Batha £ Fès' best budget option. Expect, clean and simple rooms with no frills. ⓐ Place de l'Istiqlal Batha ⓣ 035 74 10 77

Marrakech
Hotel Gallia £ Very central and clean establishment that gets booked up at least a month in advance. ⓐ 30 Rue de la Recette ⓣ 024 44 59 13 ⓦ www.ilove-marrakesh.com/hotelgallia

Meknès
Palais Didi £££ Restored 18th-century palace stuffed with antiques and located smack-dab next to Bab Mansour. ⓐ 7 Dar el Kbira ⓣ 035 55 85 90 ⓦ www.palaisdidi.com

Ouarzazate
Berbere Palace £££ Every amenity possible at this luxurious five-star property made up of air-conditioned bungalows. ⓐ Quartier Mansour Eddahbi ⓣ 024 88 31 05

Rabat
Hotel Central £ Exactly what the title says – a central hotel.
ⓐ Rue al-Basra ⓣ 037 70 73 56

Tangier
Hotel Continental £ Built in 1865, this is Morocco's oldest hotel. It maintains a quaint charm that speaks of its former glory.
ⓐ 36 Dar Baroud ⓣ 039 93 10 24

Tétouan
Hotel Regina £ Dated but clean place to rest your head for cheap.
ⓐ 8 Rue Sidi Mandri ⓐ 039 96 21 13

RIADS/GUESTHOUSES
Fès
Riyad Scheherazade £££ If you've got the cash, splurge at this converted palace. ⓐ 23 Arsat Bennis Douh ⓣ 035 74 16 42 ⓦ www.sheheraz.com

Marrakech
Nejma Lounge £ This new riad charms due to its liberal use of colour and buzzy atmosphere. ⓐ 45 Derb Sidi M'hamed El Haj, Bab Doukkala ⓣ 024 38 23 41 ⓦ www.riad-nejmalounge.com

Rabat
Riad Oudaya £££ French-run guesthouse in the heart of the Medina.
ⓐ 46 Rue Sidi Fateh ⓣ 037 70 23 92 ⓦ www.riadoudaya.com

Preparing to go

GETTING THERE

The cheapest way to get to Morocco is to book a package holiday with
one of the leading tour operators. Tour operators specialising in Morocco
offer flight-only or flight and accommodation packages at bargain prices.

By air

Royal Air Maroc (RAM) flies from London Heathrow to Casablanca,
Marrakech and Tangier, and has direct flights from New York to
Casablanca, as well as connecting flights to all other Moroccan cities
(Ⓦ www.royalairmaroc.com). **GB Airways** flies from London Heathrow to
Marrakech, **Atlas Blue** (Ⓦ www.atlas-blue.com) flies from London
Gatwick to Marrakech, and **British Airways** flies from London Gatwick to
Agadir and Marrakech and from London Heathrow to Fès, Casablanca
and Tangier. Other airlines flying to Morocco include **Thomsonfly**
(Manchester to Agadir and Manchester to Marrakech via London Luton
Ⓦ www.thomsonfly.com), **easyJet** (London Gatwick to Marrakech
Ⓦ www.easyjet.com), Lufthansa (London Heathrow to Casablanca via
Frankfurt, Germany Ⓦ www.lufthansa.com) and **Air France**
(London Heathrow to Marrakech Ⓦ www.airfrance.com).

   Many people are aware that air travel emits CO_2, which contributes
to climate change. You may be interested in the possibility of lessening
the environmental impact of your flight through the charity Climate
Care, which offsets your CO_2 by funding environmental projects around
the world. Visit Ⓦ www.climatecare.org

By ship

The most frequent ferries run from Algeciras in Spain to Tangier or
Ceuta. Ferries operate less frequently in winter.

Comarit ⓐ Corner of Avenue des F.A.R. and Rue de Marseille, Tangier
ⓣ 00 212 39 32 00 32 Ⓦ www.comarit.com

Euroferrys ⓐ Viajes Eurotras, SA, Avenida de la Marina, 11201 Algeciras
ⓣ 00 34 956 65 23 24 Ⓦ www.euroferrys.com

By rail

Sleepers depart daily from Paris to Madrid (13 hours), where passengers must change trains for Algeciras (11 hours). The **Thomas Cook Overseas Timetable** gives details of many rail, bus and shipping services worldwide, and will help you plan a rail journey to, from and around Morocco. It is available in the UK from some stations, or at any branch of Thomas Cook (🕻 01733 416477 ⓦ www.thomascookpublishing.com).

TOURISM AUTHORITY

The **Moroccan National Tourist Board**, based in London, offers good advice. ⓐ 205 Regent St, London W1B 4HB 🕻 020 7437 0073 ⓔ mnto@morocco-tourism.com ⓦ www.visitmorocco.org

BEFORE YOU LEAVE
Health and prescriptions

There are no mandatory vaccination requirements other than to keep tetanus and polio immunisation up to date. Medical insurance is advisable for travel to Morocco, which is usually offered as part of a travel insurance package.

Take regular prescription medicines with you to ensure you don't run out. Pack a small first-aid kit with the usuals, and consider a dental check before you go if you are planning an extended stay in Morocco. Emergency dental treatment will be available in most tourist resorts. Ask your hotel receptionist or your tour operator rep to recommend a dentist.

ENTRY FORMALITIES

Check well before you travel that your **passport** is up to date and has at least three months to run before it expires. For the latest information in the UK on how to renew your passport, and the processing times, contact the **Passport Agency** (🕻 0870 521 0410 ⓦ www.ukpa.gov.uk). All children, including newborn babies, require their own passport, unless they are included on the passport of the person they are travelling with.

British, EU, US, Canadian and Scandinavian passport holders can stay up to three months without a visa. Australian, New Zealand and South

African passport holders need a visa, which can be obtained at the point of arrival into Morocco. All categories of traveller must have a full passport (British Visitor's Passports are not valid). Other nationalities need to obtain a visa from the Moroccan consulate in their country of residence before departure. Israeli nationals are not permitted to enter Morocco.

Customs

Duty free goods of the following values and amounts may be brought into Morocco hassle-free: 400 g of loose tobacco, 200 cigarettes or 50 cigars and 1 l of alcohol. Animals can be brought into Morocco, but you will need a medical certificate and an anti-rabies certificate.

Drugs

Historically, most of the marijuana exported to Europe originated in Morocco. Recently authorities have been cracking down and those caught in possession face prison sentences. Do not, under any circumstances, accept packages from strangers, and avoid the *kif*-growing areas of the Rif in the northern part of the country.

MONEY

The local currency is the dirham (DH). It is not quoted on international markets and it is what is called a soft currency, so the rate is set by the Moroccan government. The dirham is divided into 100 centimes. In some places, the locals refer to centimes as francs. The importation or exportation of Moroccan currency is prohibited, so you need to change money on arrival and to change all your dirham when you leave. Only change what you need during the last few days of your holiday and don't leave it to the last minute, as you won't get the best rate of exchange at airports. Unlimited foreign currency or traveller's cheques can be brought into the country.

In the tourist areas, there are plenty of exchange bureaux and banks, and most banks in the major cities and tourist resorts have ATMs (cash machines). In the main resorts, you can usually find one that will accept your debit card and you can take money directly out of your account

INSURANCE

Check that your insurance policy covers you adequately for loss of possessions and valuables, for activities you might want to try – say horse riding or watersports – and for emergency medical and dental treatment, including flights home, if required. Note that UK visitors are not entitled to reduced-cost or free medical treatment, as Morocco is not part of the EU.

back home. In some towns, though, you may have to use your credit card, because not all of the local banks will recognise your debit card. Major credit cards are widely accepted in most hotels and shops, but some restaurants still do not accept them, so you should always carry some cash. It is better to pay in cash if you want to buy anything in any of the traditional markets, as you are sure to get a much better price.

CLIMATE

Morocco has a diverse landscape and temperatures vary widely depending on the terrain. In general, temperatures during the high season tend to be very hot (up to 40°C/104°F), unless you are on the coast with a cooling sea breeze. In the desert, even at the warmest times of year, nights can be much cooler. In spring and autumn, temperatures tend to be more bearable in the interior and the desert, but much cooler in the mountains or by the sea, so you may need extra clothing if you are travelling to these locations. In the High Atlas, there is snow for most of the year.

BAGGAGE ALLOWANCE

Baggage allowances vary according to the airline, destination and the class of travel, but 20 kg (44 lb) per person is the norm for luggage that is carried in the hold. You are allowed one item of cabin baggage weighing no more than 5 kg (11 lb), and measuring 46 by 30 by 23 cm (18 by 12 by 9 in). In addition, you can carry your duty free purchases as hand baggage. Be sure to limit your carry-on liquids as you can only take on board bottles of liquids placed in a small, clear plastic bag with no more than 100 ml inside.

During your stay

AIRPORTS

Most Moroccan airports are served by reasonably good roads, but if you are driving yourself, remember to allow plenty of time to reach the airport when flying back home. Taxis offer the quickest alternative – but be sure to get only a licensed taxi to your destination. Public transport is also available, but you should keep an eye on your possessions at all times as pickpocketing is common.

For details of flight arrivals and departures when in Morocco, contact **National Airports Administration** (ⓐ Autoroute de Settat, Casablanca ❶ 022 43 78 07 Ⓦ www.onda.org.ma) – note the website is in French.

BEACHES

In summer, many beaches have lifeguards and a safety flag system. If you are on one of the Atlantic beach resorts, such as Agadir or Essaouira, you need to be aware there can be quite strong underwater currents.

COMMUNICATIONS

Phones

It is cheapest to make phone calls from public phone boxes, taxiphone shops or telephones in post offices. International calls made from hotel rooms are prohibitively expensive. You will need lots of change for call boxes. Some of the taxiphone shops (in most resort areas) let you pay for the call after you make it.

Mobile phones

Most mobile phones will work in Morocco if you have a roaming service by picking up a local network. Mobile phone charges can be expensive for a call from abroad, but texting is the cheapest way to communicate.

Postal services

The postal system is fairly efficient, and most towns will have a post office. You can usually arrange Poste Restante facilities if you need to.

Post offices are typically open 08.00–13.00 Mon–Sat summer, 08.00–12.00 & 14.00–18.00 Mon–Fri, 08.00–12.00 Sat winter. Small postcards and letters cost 8DH to the UK, 11DH to Canada and the USA or 14DH to Australia.

Internet access
Morocco is well-connected to the internet and there are plenty of cybercafés throughout the country serving the population. Per hour costs usually run between 5 and 10DH.

CUSTOMS
Shopping and bartering
When browsing the bazaars, do not begin bartering with the seller unless you have a genuine interest in making a purchase. The barter process is all part of the fun, but if you settle on a price, you will be expected to pay for it. Purchasing a carpet is an even lengthier affair, often involving many cups of mint tea and unfurling of rugs. Take your time and do not rush.

Eating and drinking
Other than during Ramadan, food and drink can be purchased and eaten throughout the day. In fact, it's at night when the best food sellers come out to sell their wares in the public squares. Pull up a seat on one of the benches to enjoy your dinner; however, if the seats are full and a woman approaches, you will be expected to give up your chair.

When things don't go your way
Moroccans are very passionate people and they love a good chat in the street. If ever anything goes wrong on your travels, do not shout as the Moroccans will not be impressed. Instead, stay calm and firmly insist on seeing management staff members to get your problems sorted.

DRESS CODES
In most resorts, the dress code is pretty relaxed. As a show of respect, it is

best to cover up more revealing beach clothing when you go to eat in a restaurant. Topless sunbathing is rare, mainly confined to the beaches of Agadir. When visiting major cities, men are advised to wear trousers or long shorts – especially if visiting a historical sight of religious interest. Women should wear skirts or trousers that fall below the knee and shirts or blouses that cover the shoulders (preferably also the elbow) to avoid stares. Headscarfs are useful for women, as they should be worn when entering religious buildings. They are available to borrow, but you may prefer to bring your own.

ELECTRICITY

Voltage is 220V/50Hz, which is compatible with the UK. Sockets take the European-style, round, two-pin plugs. You will need an adaptor if you are from the UK or Ireland – you can buy one in the airport. If you are buying electrical appliances to take home, always check that they will work at home before you make your purchase.

EMBASSIES & CONSULATES

British Consulate 📍 40 Boulevard d'Anfa, Casablanca 📞 022 36 02 74
British Consulate 📍 55 Boulevard Terktouni, Residence Taib, Marrakech 📞 044 43 50 95
British Embassy 📍 17 Boulevard de la Tour Hassan, Rabat 📞 037 63 62 10/ 23 86 00 ✉ british@mtds.com 🌐 www.britain.org.ma
British Consulate 📍 9 Rue d'Amérique du Sud, Tangier 📞 039 93 69 39
US Consulate 📍 8 Boulevard Moulay Youssef, Casablanca 📞 022 26 45 50
US Embassy 📍 2 Avenue de Mohammed el Fassi, Rabat 📞 037 76 22 65 🌐 www.rabat.usembassy.gov

MEDICAL EMERGENCIES

English-speaking doctors are easily found in Morocco at most clinics and hospitals. If in doubt, ask for a list of local English-speaking health professionals from your concierge or get one sent, faxed or emailed to you from your embassy.

> **EMERGENCY NUMBERS**
> In the case of an emergency, try to find someone who speaks
> French or Arabic nearby to help get the message across quickly.
> **Police ❶** 19 (in towns); 177 (outside towns) **Fire ❶** 16
> **Ambulance ❶** 15

GETTING AROUND

Buses

There are many private networks competing for business in Morocco and
there is an extensive service. **CTM** (ⓐ Exit km 13½, Autoroute
Casablanca–Rabat ❶ 022 45 80 80) has a national service and modern,
comfortable buses (usually), but often has a separate bus station. Most
towns will have a central bus station, which can be a chaotic place filled
with touts, full of timetable information. **Supratours** has a service that
links with the trains for access to the south of the country (ⓐ 16 Rue
Abderrahmane el Ghafiki, Rabat ❶ 037 77 65 20).

Car hire

Car hire is expensive in Morocco. The cheapest deals for car hire are
usually available on the internet. It is best to book a car before you leave.
All the main international companies have representatives in Morocco,
including **Avis** (ⓦ www.avis.com); **Hertz** (ⓦ www.hertz.com); **Europcar**
(ⓦ www.europcar.com); and **Budget** (ⓦ www.budget.com). Local hire
companies sometimes offer cheaper deals, but there is no guarantee of
the quality of service. Car seats for babies or infants can be a bit of a
lottery unless you book in advance. In some resorts you can hire a moped.
You need to be a fairly confident driver, be of the required age and have all
necessary documentation, including a motorcycle licence.

Driving

To drive a car or motorbike in Morocco you must be over 21 and possess
a full driving licence. It is a good idea to have your passport with you,
especially if your driving licence doesn't have photo identity.

Always check that the spare tyre is in good condition, and try the brakes if possible. The only legally required insurance is third party, but it is advisable to take out the extra Collision Damage Waiver and Personal Accident insurance to cover all eventualities.

In the event of an emergency, contact the nearest police post. You will find police road checks are standard throughout Morocco, and you can be asked for your driving papers. You will likely be waved on when they spot you are a tourist. If you are bringing a car from Europe, make sure your insurance includes a Green Card covering Morocco. If it does not, you will be able to buy insurance on arriving at frontier posts; apart from Green Cards, insurance policies are not valid unless issued by a company with an office in Morocco. The Moroccan Insurance Bureau is **Bureau Central Marocain des Sociétés d'Assurances** (ⓐ 100 Rue Mostafa el Manni, Casablanca ⓣ 022 39 28 57 ⓔ bcma-sec@casanet.ma).

Everywhere you stop, someone will appear offering to 'guard' your vehicle. These attendants are the Moroccan equivalent of the parking

⬤ *Enjoy a ride in a calèche*

meter and a vital part of the local economy; 3DH is a usual fee for daytime parking for a few hours; 5–10DH for overnight parking.

Four-star petrol and diesel are widely available. Unleaded (*sans plomb*) is not the norm but becoming more common. If you are travelling to remote areas, especially in the south, fill up before you leave urban areas.

Morocco is updating its road system, with many new motorways being built. The national motorway (*autoroute nationale*), given an 'N' notation, runs between most major cities and includes some toll roads. Smaller roads have 'P' and 'R' notations. In winter some mountain passes may be blocked by snow. In spring, beware flash floods in river valleys, especially in the High Atlas and the south. Further information is available from the **Touring Club of Morocco** (ⓐ 3 Avenue des Far, Casablanca ⓣ 022 27 13 04). Speed limits are 100 km (60 miles) an hour outside towns, 40 km (24 miles) an hour within town limits.

The bus service and *louage* (shared taxis) are the best way to cover large distances and to places where the train doesn't go. Taxis are the easiest way to get from your hotel to the airport and around the city centres. The most important thing to do is to take an official yellow taxi and to ensure that your driver uses the meter. At night, the rate may be increased by 50 per cent and you can be charged extra for luggage. *Grands taxis*, usually Mercedes and also called *louage*, shuttle a number of passengers over greater distances, usually between cities.

Trains
ONCF, the national rail service, has an efficient and comfortable service, but it is not very extensive and only goes as far south as Marrakech. ⓦ www.oncf.org.ma

HEALTH, SAFETY & CRIME
Stomach upset is a common complaint and usually passes in a few hours. It has a variety of minor causes, including exposure to bugs not common at home or spicy food. The best policy when trying to avoid more serious stomach problems is to eat in good and clean cafés, restaurants and hotels. Spending a little more is worthwhile, to avoid

being ill for a day or two on your holiday. This is especially important when you are eating shellfish, chicken and salads. Women who are pregnant or breastfeeding should take particular care in where and what they eat. If you do get a stomach bug and diarrhoea, you will need to rest. Drink lots of water and take rehydration preparations to replace the fluids you lose. If the symptoms persist for longer than 48 hours, then ask your holiday rep or your hotel reception staff to recommend a doctor, as you will need to take medication.

The sun is very strong in Morocco and the presence of a coastal breeze often means you can burn before you know it. Young children and people with fair skin can get badly sunburnt, so liberal use of strong sunscreen and covering up with loose-fitting clothing and especially a hat is recommended. Sunstroke can ruin your holiday, so don't try to get a good suntan in the first few days. If you're taking a young family, it is best to avoid the months of July and August if you can. Morocco is a very hot and dry country so you must drink lots of water (always stick to bottled) to keep hydrated, especially if you do sport, are walking in the middle of the day or taking an excursion into the desert. Avoid drinking too much alcohol, as this will cause dehydration. Extreme dehydration can make you seriously ill, so drink more water than you think you need!

Moroccan pharmacies are well-stocked, particularly in the resort areas and the major cities. Medical services in urban areas are highly competent. All pharmacists speak French; few speak English although local tourist offices will be able to direct you to an English-speaking chemist. If you are holidaying with a baby, the usual brands of disposable nappies are available, as are babyfood and most common medicines. Bring a stock of your usual powdered baby milk if your infant has fussy tastes or if you are concerned that he or she will react to local products. Pack any medications or creams your baby needs with you. Changing facilities are not readily available in towns and cities and you need to improvise.

Crime rates in Morocco are quite low, but care is advised in big cities, where petty theft and pickpocketing are common. Women should be careful when travelling alone – strict restraints on local women, combined with widespread pornographic material of Western origin, mean Moroccan men have a sadly distorted view of the 'availability' of Western females. Morocco has also traditionally attracted many homosexual visitors and in recent years the number of young men offering sex for money has increased – males travelling alone are often assumed to be in Morocco for that sole reason.

On some tourist beaches, there are special tourist police to ensure you have a safe and enjoyable holiday. But you should always be wary of pickpockets, especially in places where there are a lot of distractions and young people who seem to be just hanging around. Beware *faux guides*, or false guides, in Morocco (see page 43).

In the event of hassle, engage the help of passers-by – shouting '*chouma*' (sh-ow-ma) or the equivalent English word '*shame*' often does the trick. Most Moroccans will come to your aid if they see you are in trouble. If you find yourself with an overpersistent 'guide', head for a policeman – such insistent bothering of tourists is illegal and the tout will soon vanish.

It is now safe to travel to the Western Sahara, following peace accords signed with *Polisario* rebels. It is still best to avoid the remoter areas of the Rif, where *kif* cultivation is still prevalent.

MEDIA

British and French newspapers are available in big cities. Both the *International Herald Tribune* and the *Guardian Weekly* are usually easy to find. Local press is divided between French and Arabic dailies. The main French papers are the pro-government *Le Matin Du Sahara*, the opposition *L'Opinion* and the communist *Al-Bayanne*. Of the Arabic papers, *Al-Alam*, loyal to the Istiqlal party, has the widest circulation.

BBC World Service is theoretically found on short wave 15.07 mHz and 17.705 mHz. Most large hotels have satellite TV, receiving CNN News and European Sky News. Moroccan television broadcasts many programmes in French. International news sources can also be downloaded off the internet – there is no censorship of international online resources in Morocco.

OPENING HOURS

The rise in low-cost travel has brought a subsequent boom in tourism numbers to Morocco. As such, attractions are starting to adhere to stricter opening hours in order to accommodate the needs of visitors. Most attractions open 09.00–17.00 with at least an hour set aside in the middle of the day for lunch. Closures can be expected on Friday afternoons and Saturday mornings for religious sights.

Banks

These can be erratic. The official opening hours for banks are 08.00–11.30 Mon–Fri summer, 08.00–11.30 Mon–Thur, 13.30–16.30 Fri winter. In tourist areas it is likely the banks will be open for longer hours. Exchange bureaux will probably be open 08.00–20.00 in tourist resorts, but closed for a time on Fridays.

Shops and restaurants

As most shops and restaurants are family owned, opening hours are subject to the whims of the management. During national holidays and summer months, shops might decide to shut when the owners go away for a break. Restaurants can also shut unexpectedly if a personal guest or family member comes to visit. If in doubt, try calling ahead. Friday nights and Saturday mornings are the usual times when last-minute closures result.

TELEPHONING MOROCCO

To call Morocco from the UK, dial 00 212 followed by the remaining eight-digit number (minus the inital zero).

TELEPHONING ABROAD

To call an overseas number from Morocco, dial 00 and wait for a second dialling tone, then dial the country code (UK = 44) and the area code (minus the initial 0) followed by the number.

RELIGION

Islam is the country's religion and it has an important impact on the way people behave. One of the distinct sounds of Morocco is the Muezzin's call to prayer from the minaret towers of the mosques. Morocco is a liberal Muslim country and extremist Islamic groups are banned. There is a more relaxed attitude to religion than in the neighbouring countries of Algeria and Libya, and women have more freedom in how they dress.

For many Moroccans, their religious belief is the most important part of their life, so you should respect this. In most cases, you are only allowed into the outer courtyard areas of the mosques, and only when it is not time for prayer. You will not be allowed into the prayer halls. The month of Ramadan is the most important time in the religious calendar (see page 104). It usually falls sometime around late November to early January, depending on the lunar calendar. Restaurants and cafés are all likely to be shut during the day as the locals fast during daylight hours for the whole month, but in the evening the place buzzes with life.

TIME DIFFERENCES

Morocco is one hour ahead of Greenwich Mean Time. This means that when it is noon in Morocco, it is 11am in London, 6am in New York (EST), 3am in Los Angeles (PST), noon in Western Europe, 10pm (11pm during daylight saving) in Sydney and midnight in Auckland.

TIPPING

Tipping for a service is the norm in Morocco. You should carry some small change around with you. Guides, waiters and park attendants will all expect a tip. Add about an extra 10 per cent to a bill to tip a waiter. This will be expected despite being on top of a service charge.

TOILETS

You should be able to use the public toilets in a restaurant or café. They vary in their level of cleanliness, so make a judgement about the place first before you ask to use the toilet. You should always carry some toilet paper with you as it is rarely supplied.

TRAVELLERS WITH DISABILITIES

Morocco is a difficult country for visitors with disabilities, as it is only the big, modern hotels that have proper, specially adapted facilities. Most of the moderately priced to higher-end hotels have lift, or elevator, services and some, like the Jnan Palace in Fès, have installed wheelchair ramps. Wheelchairs are available at all international airports. Contact the Moroccan National Tourist Office for information on your destination.

WOMEN TRAVELLERS

Women occasionally have problems with harassment from males in Arab countries. To avoid this unwanted attention, avoid entering cafés on your own, and try to dress fairly conservatively. Be wary that signs and body language may portray different messages than they would back home. Wearing provocative beachwear away from the beach and on the streets is likely to lead to problems.

WEIGHTS & MEASURES

Imperial to metric

1 inch = 2.54 centimetres
1 foot = 30 centimetres
1 mile = 1.6 kilometres
1 ounce = 28 grams
1 pound = 454 grams
1 pint = 0.6 litres
1 gallon = 4.6 litres

Metric to imperial

1 centimetre = 0.4 inches
1 metre = 3 feet, 3 inches
1 kilometre = 0.6 miles
1 gram = 0.04 ounces
1 kilogram = 2.2 pounds
1 litre = 1.8 pints

ACKNOWLEDGEMENTS

The publishers would like to thank the following individuals and organisations for providing their photographs for this book, to whom the copyright belongs:

Daniel Boiteau/Dreamstime.com page 107; Radoslaw Botev/Wikimedia Commons page 74; Robert Holmes/Corbis page 79; Author's Image/Tips Images page 10; Shawn Lipowski/Wikimedia Commons page 75; Morocco National Tourist Office page 52; Photononstop/Tips Images pages 37, 95; Pictures Colour Library pages 13, 57; Alessandro Da Tos/Tips Images page 118; Sandro Vannini/Corbis page 86; K.M. Westermann/Corbis page 82; Wikimedia Commons page 76; World Pictures/Photoshot pages 16, 28, 34, 92, 103; all the rest Thomas Cook Tour Operations.

Project editor: Alison Coupe
Layout: Donna Pedley
Proofreader: Karolin Thomas
Indexer: Amanda Jones

Send your thoughts to
books@thomascook.com

- Found a beach bar, peaceful stretch of sand or must-see sight that we don't feature?
- Like to tip us off about any information that needs a little updating?
- Want to tell us what you love about this handy, little guidebook and more importantly how we can make it even handier?

Then here's your chance to tell all! Send us ideas, discoveries and recommendations today and then look out for your valuable input in the next edition of this title.

Email to the above address or write to:
HotSpots Series Editor, Thomas Cook Publishing, PO Box 227, Unit 9, Coningsby Road, Peterborough PE3 8SB, UK.